# WHAT THEY NEVER TOLD US... ABOUT HOW TO GET ALONG WITH EACH OTHER

## JUDSON EDWARDS

**HARVEST HOUSE PUBLISHERS**
Eugene, Oregon 97402

**WHAT THEY NEVER TOLD US ABOUT
HOW TO GET ALONG WITH EACH OTHER**

Copyright © 1991 by Harvest House Publishers
Eugene, Oregon 97402

Library of Congress Cataloging-in-Publication Data

Edwards, Judson.
    What they never told us about how to get along with each other / Judson
    Edwards.
    ISBN 0-89081-882-7
    1. Interpersonal relations—Religious aspects—Christianity. 2. Christian life—1960. I. Title.
    BV4597.52.E38    1991
    158'.2—dc20                             91-9692
                                                    CIP

*For Laurie and L.T.*

# ♥ CONTENTS ♥

# WHAT THEY NEVER TOLD US... ABOUT HOW TO GET ALONG WITH EACH OTHER

# 1

# *Worlds in Collision*

*very relationship is a collision.*
Back in the seventies, Kenny Rogers and Dottie West sang a popular duet that reminded us of that truth. The song lamented the collapse of a relationship between a man and a woman who had once shared a deep love. Their relationship had great promise; they were looking forward to years of bliss together. But the relationship fell apart, leaving both parties hurt and stunned. The last line of the chorus pinpointed the reason for the failure: "That's what happens when two worlds collide."

Every time we enter into a relationship with another person, two worlds collide. We bring to that relationship our own unique world: our experiences, temperament, family background, religious heritage, style of relating to people, taste for food and music and entertainment, and so on. And the other person brings his or her unique world to that relationship as well. The collision, then, is inevitable, for no two of us ever come from identical worlds.

All too often, the collision is a devastating crash like the one described in the song. A marriage disintegrates. Children become estranged from their parents. Friends become enemies. Churches split. Brothers feud with brothers, and sisters gossip about sisters. All we have to do is look around us to see the devastating results of colliding worlds.

Tragically, most of us can see the devastation in our own experience. I think it fair to say that most of the pain in our lives is caused by poor relationships. We may rail against God because some natural disaster has harmed us. We may be upset because some awful disease has attacked our body. We may be uptight because the stock we bought so confidently last year has suddenly plummeted. But most of us can add up all the pain caused by such circumstances, and it will not come close to equaling the pain we feel because our relationships are bad.

The most persistent misery we have is caused by:

- The bitterness we feel toward our parents for some of the things they did to us when we were young.

- The estrangement we're experiencing from our husband or wife.

- The gulf that is developing between us and our children.

- The growing hostility we feel toward the people at the office.

- The lingering resentment we feel toward a former spouse.

- The lack of closeness we have with *anyone*.

The list could go on indefinitely, but suffice it to say that if we could just repair our relationships, our joy-level would rise immeasurably.

## The Art of Tender Collisions

In the face of such destruction it's easy to just shrug our shoulders and sigh, "That's what happens when two worlds collide." But in this book I'm going to suggest another response to you. Instead of feeling helplessly trapped in a series of bad relationships, I'm going to propose that we learn the art of tender collisions. True, no one is from our exact world (which, by the way, always makes them look wrong to us). True, every relationship we have will involve a collision of some sort. But that collision doesn't have to be an abrasive, destructive one. We can learn the art of *tender* collisions, and in the process learn to love people more.

Colliding tenderly with people is an art, however—an art that must be learned. Most of us have learned our relational skills from an assortment of unofficial teachers—parents, grandparents, friends, bosses, television heroes, and so forth. Those teachers never gave us an official course in relationships, but we picked up our relational habits from them just by observing them in the normal affairs of life.

Though we are reluctant even yet to admit it, some of those role models for relationships were none too exemplary. They themselves have had a series of destructive collisions throughout their lives, but we doggedly follow them anyway, content to believe that they are experts at establishing and sustaining quality relationships. It's a classic case of the blind leading the blind.

If nothing else, I hope this book will force you to look at your basic style of relating to people. As difficult as it may be to admit it, it is distinctly possible that the way you have done it all your life is not good enough. If you stay on the current course, you are destined for even more painful collisions—and even more misery.

This book will explore a new way of relating to people. Or, maybe better said, it will explore an old way of relating to people that we either have never known or have somehow forgotten. It is not enough, you see, to want better relationships or to yearn for more love. *Wanting and yearning are useless unless they prompt us to act, to change, to treat people differently.* This book will suggest some specific actions we can take to make our relationships better. It is, I hope, a practical guide for making all future collisions more tender.

## Correcting Our Misconceptions

Along the way we will probe some misconceptions we might have about relating to others. These misconceptions have been handed to us by our unofficial teachers, popular psychology, and even popular religion, but they are false nonetheless and lead us away from loving relationships. If we're following a faulty map, how can we ever arrive at where we want to be? I hope to show you how we have taken some wrong turns on the road to successful relationships so that we can correct our map, retrace our steps, and head in a new direction.

Just to prepare you for what is ahead, let me give you a quick test. Do you agree or disagree with these statements?

1. The most important ingredient we can bring to a relationship is healthy self-esteem.

2. It is healthy and good to express anger to another person.

3. We should always expect supreme effort and high achievement from the people around us.

4. A parent's job is to keep a child from failing and to make sure the child becomes successful.

5. We should always be fair in our dealings with people.

6. The more people we love, the better.

7. We best communicate our love to people by telling them we love them.

8. Any relationship can be rejuvenated if we will take it seriously.

9. We learn to love better by studying psychology and finding out the intricacies of the human psyche.

I am going to suggest to you that there is a flaw in each of those statements, a flaw that just might be sabotaging your attempt to build relationships that are loving and lasting. If you agree with any of those statements, I hope you'll stick with me through this book. I may be able to change your mind, and in doing so change the way you relate to people. (Actually, if you disagree with all of the above statements, I hope you'll stick with me too. You're obviously a keen student of human affairs and most definitely a kindred spirit.)

## A Note to Browsers

Occasionally an editor will ask a writer, "Who is your intended audience? What kind of reader are you trying to reach in your book?" Those seem to me to be fair questions—not only for an editor to ask, but also for a person browsing through a book to ask. When I'm flipping through a book at a bookstore and trying to decide if that book is worth my hard-earned cash, the questions I'm trying to answer are: "Is this book aimed at me? Does it speak to my situation? Can it sustain my interest?" If the answers are yes, the book is worth the cover price and more. If the answers are no, the book is a waste of money even if it sits on the sale table.

So if you're browsing through this book and trying to decide if it's for you, I'll try to make your job easier by telling you my target audience.

• This book is for those who have had some recent relational jolts and are growing weary of the stress they're experiencing because of other people. They're tired of harsh collisions, and would like them to be more tender.

• This book is also for those who feel trapped in a relationship—trapped in a dull marriage, trapped in a negative situation with a child, trapped in any kind of relationship that is going in the wrong direction. There are some specific things we can do to energize a sagging relationship, and this book is about those things.

• This book is for people who are happy in their marriage, happy with their children, happy with their lives. But they want to protect and enhance their relationships to keep them from deteriorating over time.

• This book is for people who are at least slightly disillusioned with "revolutionary new ideas" and who wonder if some of the old ways were not more truthful. While I have tried to stay current with regard to recent psychological and ecclesiastical trends, I must confess that I am more enamored with "old" truth than with "new" truth. Most of the ideas in this book are at least as old as the New Testament.

• This book is for people who are nonconformists, people who will dare to relate to others in an unconventional manner. If we begin to put some of the ideas in this book into practice, we might be labeled naive, unsophisticated, old-fashioned, or even silly. If these ideas take us to a deeper level of love, though, I think you'll agree that being scorned by the sophisticates is a small price to pay.

## Eyes to See

When I was in the fourth grade, I had an experience that has become for me a parable of what happens to us in our relationships. In the fourth grade I got my first pair of glasses, and I can remember to this day the shock I felt when I tried those glasses on. I looked out the window of the optometrist's office and couldn't believe what I saw. The trees had distinct leaves on them! The signs had distinct letters on them! People, even at a distance, had distinct faces on them! I was amazed at what I saw when I looked at the world through those glasses.

I was amazed because gradually, imperceptibly, my vision had become fuzzy. I didn't realize my vision was fuzzy, of course. In fact, I assumed everyone saw the world just the way I did, that everyone saw fuzzy leaves, letters, and faces. When I slipped those glasses on, I was shocked because I realized what I had been missing. As I said, I can still remember the feeling of surprise I had when I looked out at the world through "new eyes."

Something like that happens to us in our relationships. Gradually, imperceptibly, our way of seeing people becomes fuzzy. We've grown accustomed to treating the people in our lives a certain way and assume that this way is best. We just "rock along" in our relational habits, treating our husband the way we've always treated him, treating our kids the way our parents treated us, treating people in general the way we've been taught by our unofficial teachers. Occasionally we may wonder why our relationships are not richer, or why we bounce off people like a pinball clanging through an arcade machine. But we never stop to think that the problem is with *us*— that our way of relating to people is fuzzy and wrong.

I'm hoping this book can do for us what those glasses did for me back in the fourth grade. I'm hoping to remind all of us just how good our relationships can be, to correct our misconceptions so that we won't settle for second best with the people we're supposed to love. If someone reads something in these pages and feels the same awe and surprise I felt when I looked out the optometrist's window, I will count the book a whopping success.

Jesus often said, after one of his teaching sessions, "He who has ears to hear, let him hear." It was a way of reminding his listeners that not everyone with ears actually hears, that not everyone who heard what he had to say would receive the truth of it or respond to it. I learned in the fourth grade that what is true of ears is true of eyes, too: Not everyone who has eyes can actually see.

So let me do a slight twist on Jesus' ancient line and offer you my wish as you read this book and try to look honestly at the quality of your relationships: He who has eyes to see, let him see.

# 2

# *The Most Important Question*

*It is entirely possible that our relationships are poor not because we have latent hostility in our psyche, not because our self-image is bad, and not because our potty training was mishandled. It is possible that our relationships are poor simply because we have not made the decision to deny self and serve the other person.*

We might as well bite the bullet and admit up front that there is one primary reason our relationships are suffering: We are too full of "self." I hate to be that blunt about it, but I know it is true, and so, in your heart of hearts, do you. We can't love others because we are selfish. Our ego is too big. We go into our relationships expecting others to "meet our needs." The spotlight always shines on those three words that are sweeter to us than any others: "I" and "me" and "my."

19

Because of our bent toward selfishness, the advice of Jess Lair in his book *I Ain't Much, Baby, But I'm All I've Got*, is crucial if we want to revitalize our relationships:

> One basic idea is: If there is a problem here, I caused it. This runs exactly contrary to what you want to believe. I've got news for you. It runs exactly contrary to what I want to believe, too. But I don't really have that much choice. My experience, my own story, has led me to believe that if there is a problem here, I caused it. Now that's very sad, but in another way, it's very happy. Because it says that if there's a problem here, I had an awfully big hand, if not an exclusive hand, in causing it. So I can get to work on it.

That kind of statement, as painful as it is to make, is a forerunner to loving relationships. It is an ego-crashing, self-humiliating kind of statement that puts us in the proper frame of mind for change.

## Baby Steps Toward Self-Denial

Our culture has taught us to do many things with our "self." We have been told to assert self, love self, protect self, listen to self, respect self, and even pamper self. Our culture has not taught us, however, to do the one thing with self that Jesus made a prerequisite to following him: Deny self. "If anyone would come after me," he said, "he must deny himself. . . ." (Luke 9:23). Mention self-denial to a group of upwardly mobile, middle-class Americans, and you will get a look of disbelief. "Self-denial went out with the Puritans," the look will say. "We've moved beyond that primitive idea and now live in the enlightened age of psychology."

But the "primitive" idea of self-denial is the one we must revive if we're going to revitalize our relationships. And here, at the beginning of the book, it is the one idea we must embrace before we embrace any others. As long as self is our god, as long as everyone must march to our tune and meet our standards, any other change we make will be superficial. The root cause of our problem is *self*, and self cannot remain as it is.

So how do we learn this self-denial that is crucial to our relationships? We learn it a step at a time, through little things we say and do. We make a conscious effort to dethrone self, and that effort works its way out in seemingly insignificant events and ordinary encounters. While we like to think of self-denial as admirable and "spiritual," it is actually an arduous, unnatural process that most of us will avoid at all costs. But until we learn to deny self, we will stay stuck in relational quicksand.

In particular, there are a few simple exercises we can begin now, and these practical disciplines will take us toward both self-denial and better relationships.

• *Agree more, argue less.* The next chapter will explore this suggestion in detail, but suffice it to say now that arguing is the enemy of intimacy. We simply don't have to argue with people! About 95 percent of the issues we argue about are not worth the effort. So what if my son quotes me an erroneous baseball statistic? Is that worth arguing about? So what if my wife has had a bad day and is grumpy? Shall I ridicule her for having one bad mood? So what if the guy at the office is a pompous egomaniac? Shall I descend to his level and swap verbal punches with him? If we continually feel a need to argue with people and "straighten them out," that is a foolproof sign that self is a big problem. Every time we turn away from a potential argument, self dies a little and a relationship receives a shot of hope.

• *Listen more, talk less.* Self loves to talk, to be expert, to be in control. If we dominate most of the conversations we have, it probably is another sign that self is on a rampage. We can begin today to make a conscious effort to listen more and talk less. Self will, of course, protest and remind us of our unusual wisdom, a wisdom we should not withhold from our poor, ignorant acquaintances. But if we ignore self's pitiful cries, we will gradually put it to silence. And we will be amazed to learn that other people actually have insights too. We will also be amazed at how those people begin to enjoy our company, because while not everyone likes an incessant talker, everyone does like a genuine listener.

• *Produce more, advertise less.* Self is really in the advertising business. It loves "impressiveness" and goes out of its way to strike a marvelous public pose. Another way we deny self, then, is to quit being so concerned about "image." Erich Fromm once wrote about "the marketing character" who will do almost anything to market himself to the world. The "marketing character" wants to wear the right label, exude the right fragrance, talk the right lingo, and drive the right car. "Image" is the name of the game, and self dearly loves to play it. Is it any wonder, then, that so many relationships fail? If image is everything, then relationships are destined to be disasters. We simply cannot be "chic" all the time. By moving away from "impressiveness" and toward genuineness, we not only turn our back on a false self but we also enhance our relationships. Any relationship built on the truth has a better chance of surviving than one built on a pretty facade.

• *Confess more, accuse less.* The easiest words for self to utter are: "It's your fault." The hardest words for self to utter are: "I blew it." So, to deny self, we're going to have to say those three awful words of apology on a regular basis. Do you realize how many relationships could be salvaged right now if one of the people in the relationship would confess to wrong? Marriages could be repaired almost instantly. Grudges would be buried immediately. Churches could experience true revival overnight. But confessing and apologizing are so difficult for us that we would rather be estranged from people than swallow our pride and take some steps toward reconciliation. The key principle is: Accusation splinters relationships; confession heals them.

• *Laugh more, fret less.* You would think that self would love to laugh, but it doesn't. Self loves to worry, to fear, and to imagine awful scenarios. Left to its own devices, self will become a nervous, handwringing creature without any joy. So we deny self when we laugh. We say to it, "You are not god after all, my friend, and I'm not going to treat you with undue seriousness." When we loosen up and relax, we also do a magical thing to our relationships. It is just a fact that human beings come to life in the presence of laughter. As the Old Testament reminds us, laughter really is good medicine. In laughing more, "hanging loose" more, we heal both ourselves and those around us. I will have more to say about this later.

• *Give more, receive less.* I have called this chapter "The Most Important Question," and that question relates to our willingness to give. In just a moment I will unveil this all-important question, but let me set it up by reminding you that we enter into any relationship with one of two subconscious agendas. We either enter a relationship asking, "What can this person do for me?" Or we enter the relationship asking, "What can I do for this person?" In truth, every relationship is a mixture of both of those agendas. That is, we want to give in every relationship, and we also want to receive. But self always argues strongly for receiving. It whispers things like "Don't let her take advantage of you" and "You don't have to take that from him" and "If he doesn't start meeting your needs, you ought to leave." Self loves to say those things because self, to put it bluntly, is selfish. Left unchecked, it looks out only for number one. When we begin to give, when we focus on the other person's needs instead of our own, self writhes in anguish. It doesn't know how to handle other-centeredness. But in becoming more self-less, we make loving relationships possible.

Those six ideas seem simple and unspectacular, don't they? They certainly don't sound profound enough to make a bad relationship good. But they are! If we would begin now putting those six affirmations into our lives, we would be amazed at how quickly our relationships would improve. And the reason they are so effective is that they enable us to do precisely what Jesus said we must do if we want to follow him. They are baby steps toward self-denial.

## But What About Self-Image?

All of this emphasis on self-denial seems to fly in the face of the popular psychology that puts the emphasis on self-esteem. For years now we have been hearing that the key to good relationships is a healthy self-image. Parents and teachers have made self-esteem the prime thrust of their work with children. Preachers and writers of self-help books have joined the chorus to tell us that we should all feel good about ourselves.

In one sense the self-esteem movement has been a needed reminder that we really are created in the image of God and that we really don't have to despise ourselves. But I think it is time now to start moving back in the other direction. It is time to move beyond *self-esteem* to *self-denial*.

I would venture a guess that for every person in our society whose relationships are lousy because of a deflated self, there are ten others whose relationships are lousy because of an inflated self. For every person who needs Assertiveness Training to learn how not to be a doormat, there are ten who need Submissiveness Training to learn how not to be selfish. For every marriage that has failed because of too *little* self there are at least ten that have failed because of too *much* self! We have assumed that people need to find self and learn to feel good, when in truth they need to *lose self* and *learn to love*.

If we teach people to feel good about themselves and stop there, we have done them and the world a disservice, for we have taught them to be self-centered. But if we teach them to feel good about themselves so they can give self away, we have echoed Jesus and given them a truth that will enrich both their own lives and the world. In a certain sense, healthy self-esteem can be a necessary stop on the journey to mature personhood, but it is not the final destination. On down the road from psychology's notion of a good self-image is the Bible's "primitive" notion of loving self-denial.

## The Revolutionary Question

And now for the question which can revolutionize our relationships. If we would ask this question and then live out the answer, most of our relational difficulties would vanish immediately. The question is: *What can I do today to make life better for this particular person?*

That simple question has the power to transform any relationship because it has some explosive things going for it. I commend that question to you because, if you will dissect it carefully, you will discover five hidden truths in it that are absolutely dynamite.

*First, the question accepts responsibility for the relationship:* What can *I* do today to make life better for this particular person? It is faithful to Jess Lair's "If there is a problem here, I caused it" philosophy. The original sin in the Bible is the avoidance of responsibility. Adam said, "It wasn't my fault, God, it was Eve's." And Eve said, "It wasn't my fault, God, it was the serpent's." You and I to this very moment have it in us to say about any problem in our lives, "It's not my fault, God, it's theirs."

This question forces us to assume responsibility for our friendship, our marriage, or any other relationship we have. It does not absolve the other person in the relationship of responsibility, but it does underscore our *own* part in what the relationship has become and, even more crucial, where it is going. Granted, the "significant others" in our lives are far from perfect, but if we are content to place the blame on them and throw stones at their imperfections, we are doomed to a life of hurt and hassle. When we say "What can *I* do?" we have accepted our part in the problem and therefore our part in the solution.

*Second, the question places the emphasis on action:* What can I *do* today to make life better for this particular person? The stress falls on "doing," and that is a necessary corrective to the popular notion that love is something we "feel." Love doesn't just feel, but *acts*.

Our society seems to have forgotten that fact. It is not uncommon today for people to say they love their children—and then physically or emotionally abuse them; for husbands to say they love their wives—and then have an affair with another woman; for children to say they love their parents—and then dishonor and disobey them at every turn; for people to say they love God—and then make no attempt to know him or worship him. In our generation love has become a warm, toasty feeling detached from action. We think of love as having to do with our heart; we never think of love as having to do with our hands and feet.

The greatest definition of love ever penned—Paul's famous words in 1 Corinthians 13—is a needed antidote to the warm, toasty concept of love so prevalent today. Paul says that love does specific things, behaves in definite ways, proves itself in discernible activities: "Love is patient, love is kind. It does not envy, it does not boast, it is not proud. It is not rude, it is not self-seeking, it is not easily angered, it keeps no record of wrongs. Love does not delight in evil but rejoices with the truth. It always protects, always hopes, always perseveres." In essence, love is easy to spot, for it always comes clothed in the same garment.

When we ask ourselves "What can I *do*?" we are protesting the popular idea of love and replacing it with the biblical idea. As we will see throughout this book, there are some specific things we can do to increase the love in our lives and improve our relationships with others.

*Third, the question forces us to quit procrastinating:* What can I do *today* to make life better for this particular person? The question is current, and makes us decide *now* how we are going to behave. Relationship-repairing, it reminds us, must begin today.

No one who is emotionally healthy wants to stay trapped in a frustrating relationship. Someone trapped in a bad marriage, for instance, has every intention of improving that marriage—someday. Someone constantly fighting with her kids has every intention of bridging the generation gap and becoming close to them—someday. Someone angry at his parents for some of the sins committed against him years ago really wants to have a reconciliation—someday. But all too often "someday" never comes, and these people go to their graves estranged from those they were supposed to love.

The word "today" in the question reminds us that we can begin the painful, delightful task of improving our relationships right now. The time to act is *now*, while the relationship is still intact. We don't need any elaborate training, for the decision to love is just that—a decision. Before you finish this sentence you can decide to love your husband, or your kids, or your parents, or your friend, as never before.

*Fourth, the question denies self and places us in the role of a servant:* What can I do today *to make life better* for this particular person? The goal of the question is "to make life better" for someone else, which is the true purpose of a servant. The real genius of this question is that it forces us to take the spotlight off of self and focus it elsewhere.

A true servant specializes in the ordinary. A servant doesn't look for spectacular, headline-making activities but concentrates instead on the mundane. As we begin to ask ourselves this question, we will discover (perhaps to our disappointment) that the answer involves committing ourselves to simple chores and subtle expressions of love. "Making life better" for someone usually entails such commonplace things as delivering him coffee in bed, or giving her a kiss as you go out the door, or making a bed, or washing dishes, or any of a thousand other unspectacular deeds. Relationships rise or fall on simple actions, actions that most people see as trivial. If we hope to rejuvenate our relationships, we will have to deny self and do those trivial little acts of servanthood.

*Fifth, the question particularizes our love:* What can I do today to make life better *for this particular person?* I'm going to spend an entire chapter on this idea later in the book, so I won't steal my own thunder now and say too much. But I will remind you here that love is very narrow in its focus: We can't, and don't, love the world; we love *particular people.* A *specific person* is the one who is to get the bulk of our time, energy, money, and attention.

### Answering the Question
The question we've asked becomes revolutionary when

we're smart enough to ask it and persistent enough to answer it. As we start living the answers to the question, a sagging relationship starts coming to life.

Consider what this question could do for a stale marriage. Let's name the husband Joe and the wife Harriet, and let's say they have been married for 20 years. Three kids. Nice home in the suburbs. Plenty of money. Active in their church. From all indications, Joe and Harriet have it all.

But behind the perfect facade the world sees, Joe and Harriet know something has gone sour in their relationship. They no longer enjoy being with each other like they used to. They get irritated frequently and argue regularly. They have busied themselves working, raising the kids, maintaining the house and lawn, and doing all the other wonderful things that successful suburban families busy themselves doing. But the marriage is going flatter by the day and shows no signs of being resuscitated. Joe and Harriet have never seriously contemplated divorce, but they secretly have grown disillusioned about their marriage.

Then one day Joe decides to do something positive for the relationship. Instead of griping at Harriet for her obvious apathy and instead of suffering silently through a dying relationship, Joe decides to ask the crucial question: *What can I do today to make life better for Harriet?* It strikes him as an unsophisticated, unimpressive question, but it does seem to be practical and action-oriented, so he ponders it one morning as he is shaving and decides to try to answer it in the way he treats Harriet that day. He knows that living the answer to the question will seem unnatural and prompt him to do things he hasn't done in years, but after all, what does he have to lose?

After shaving, Joe pours Harriet a cup of coffee and brings it to her in bed, along with the morning newspaper. (Harriet, of course, immediately suspects Joe of some awful indiscretion, but that's the price you pay for neglect!) He asks her at the breakfast table what she has planned for the day, and he actually listens to her answer. When he leaves for work, he kisses her and tells her he'll be thinking about her. Midmorning, he calls Harriet just to check in and see how she's doing. When he gets home from work that afternoon, he once again gives Harriet a kiss (which means Joe has kissed Harriet more on this day than he usually does in a month). After supper, Joe helps her with the dishes (now Harriet *knows* Joe is guilty of some awful indiscretion), and asks her if she wants to walk down to the local ice cream shop for a cone. They stroll to the neighborhood Baskin-Robbins and talk about the day's activities. In bed that night Joe embraces Harriet, tells her he loves her, and, quite frankly, has her falling to sleep skeptical and confused—and a little hopeful.

Will Joe's attempts to rekindle the relationship be successful? Well, not if those attempts last just a day or two. And not if those attempts are an insincere "technique." But if they do work—if Joe persists in asking and answering the revolutionary question and Harriet responds to his love—the relationship will have been rejuvenated because the question prompted Joe to do what must be done to restore and revitalize any relationship:

• He took responsibliity for the relationship. He quit blaming God, fate, or Harriet for the bad marriage and became personally responsible.

• He took action. He quit worrying, sulking, and ignoring, and instead sprang into action. In doing so, Joe was acknowledging that his love for Harriet has more to do with how he *acts* than how he *feels*.

• He acted *now*. He took action today, which, if you think about it, is the only time we can ever do anything. We can plan and plot all we wish, but no relationship will ever be repaired unless we get off of dead center and do something *now*.

• He denied himself and tried to serve. Granted, what Joe did that day seems rather insignificant. Coffee, conversations, and kisses are hardly headline material. It would seem, in fact, that those are awfully frail tools with which to repair a floundering marriage. But they are the most effective tools imaginable if they are used consistently! In denying his big ego and trying to do small acts of servanthood, Joe was reversing that negative cycle of "I, me, and my" that dooms most relationships.

• He focused on one person. For that day, Joe made Harriet the center of his attention. Yes, he had to work, help the kids with their homework, and so on, but the question focused his attention primarily on Harriet and his relationship with her. Relationships can be healed only when we narrow our focus and love specifically.

And if Joe is serious about saving his marriage, he will keep his attention riveted on Harriet. He will begin to make self-denying love a regular practice, and he will employ the six self-denying disciplines mentioned earlier: He will agree with Harriet more and argue with her less; he will listen more and talk less; he will produce more and advertise less; he will confess more and accuse less; he will laugh more and fret less; and he will continue to give more and not be so concerned about receiving.

## In Praise of the Plain and Simple

It is entirely possible that this question which I'm saying can revolutionize any relationship will never catch on. It is so plain and simple that most modern people with even a passing knowledge of psychology will not be impressed by it. If I want the question to get serious consideration, I'm going to have to come up with an impressive name for it—something like "The Cognitive Theory of Intentional Altruism." That has a nice ring to it, doesn't it? And it will give my question an academic aura that will catch the attention of the sophisticates. Alongside Harris' Transactional Analysis, Glasser's Reality Therapy, Skinner's Behavior Modification, and Frankl's Logotherapy, we can put Edwards' Cognitive Theory of Intentional Altruism!

Sadly, we live in a day when the more complicated and obscure something is, the more profound people assume it to be. When Congress drafts a complex bill to establish a national energy policy, we are astounded at their genius. The bill would give the president "a substantial measure of administrative flexibility to draft the price regulatory mechanism in a manner designed to optimize production from domestic properties subject to a statutory parameter requiring the regulatory pattern to prevent prices from exceeding a maximum weighted average." Aren't you impressed with the lawmakers' brilliance?

One writer, severely smitten with the same communicative disease, wrote eloquently about "the elongated yellow fruit." Evidently "banana" was just too simple.

I am tired of laws that confuse citizens, insurance policies that policyholders can't comprehend, theology that people can't translate into action, and psychological theories that can't be understood and implemented by any man or woman on the street. More and more, I'm singing the praises of the plain and simple. I want to know truths I can understand and put into action. And that, in my opinion, is the strength of the question we've considered in this chapter. We can understand it, and therefore we can do something about it.

It is entirely possible that our relationships are poor not because we have latent hostility in our psyche, not because our self-image is bad, and not because our potty training was mishandled. *It is possible that our relationships are poor simply because we have not made the decision to deny self and serve the other person.* Before we go digging for deep and hidden answers, we would do well to probe the obvious.

I encourage you to give it a try. Begin to ask the simple question "What can I do today to make life better for this particular person?" and see where it takes you. You have nothing to lose, and a lifetime of loving relationships to gain.

---

*We can make our collisions tender if we deny self and consider the needs of other people before our own.*

# 3

# *How to Kill a Relationship*

*The popular idea that venting our hostility is good and therapeutic needs to be challenged. The way we have always related to people needs to be challenged too. Occasionally we need to go back to square one and ask the simple question: Is this really true?*

*I suppose I could quit writing right now*, mentioning no more ideas for making our collisions tender, and we would still have enough to work on for the rest of our lives. Learning to deny self and put the needs of another person before our own is a lifelong process that doesn't come easily or automatically to any of us. But as I mentioned at the beginning of the last chapter, dealing with a selfish self is the place to begin when we want to improve our relationships. Until we start asking the "revolutionary question," we are doomed to relational misery.

Once we have faced self, though, and made a commitment to get off the throne of the universe, we can begin to consider some specific improvements we need to make in our relationships. The rest of the book will probe definite steps we can take to make our collisions more tender. Now that we have seen that denying self is the philosophical underpinning to improving our relationships, we can move on to some practical ideas that will enable us to love better.

In this chapter I want us to think about anger—what our culture has taught us about anger, how anger affects a relationship, and what we can do to control the anger that occasionally (or frequently!) erupts from within us.

### Grandmother's Plaque

I have many wonderful memories of boyhood days spent with my grandparents in the South Texas town of Bishop. I remember spending nights in the trailer at my grandfather's cotton gin, the clatter of the machines singing me to sleep and the promise of the next day's adventures filling me with anticipation. I remember Christmas Eves where bicycles, BB guns, and Barbie dolls circled the flickering tree in the living room. I remember popcorn balls on Halloween night and baskets of glittering eggs on Easter Sunday. I remember the sound of the dominoes being shuffled by the grownups, and the smell of my grandmother's homemade rolls as they came out of the oven.

And for some strange reason I remember a plaque that my grandmother had hanging in the back bedroom. It was a plaque with a hand-stitched message on it, a message that I assume my grandmother put there with her own needle. The plaque read:

BEFORE YOU SPEAK A WORD IN ANGER
WHISPER A PRAYER
AND COUNT SLOWLY TO TEN

Why I remember the message on that plaque after 30 years I have no idea. Perhaps it burned an indelible memory on my brain because it seemed so unnecessary for my grandmother to have such a plaque. To my knowledge she never once lost her temper with me. She was always the picture of contentment and easy grace. She seemed to me almost incapable of speaking a word in anger. But now, 30 years after the plaque and 17 years after her death, I wonder: Was she really that placid? Or did she just try real hard to live by the message she had hand-stitched on that plaque?

## Out of Step with the Times

This I know for certain: The message on my grandmother's plaque is definitely out of step with the mood of our day. Whispering a prayer and counting slowly to ten sounds quaint and even silly to us. We have been taught to handle our anger in a way that includes neither prayer nor patience.

We have been taught that it is good and healthy to "vent our hostility." Psychological experts have loudly trumpeted the therapeutic value of "letting it all hang out." They have told us that expressing our anger has two positive benefits: It lets other people know exactly how we feel, and it keeps us from building up an inner reservoir of repressed hostility. In short, we should not be afraid to unleash our anger because doing so enables us to have honest relationships and a healthy psyche.

We have taken that message to heart and have become a nation of expert "hostility-venters." If our husband or wife makes a mistake that irritates us, we think nothing of unloading our frustration. If our children step out of line, we are quick to lash them with stinging words of condemnation. If an employee blows an assignment, we deem it our responsibility to shame him so he will perform better next time. After all, we owe it to others to let them know how we feel, don't we? And we owe it to ourselves to keep any hostility from building up inside us.

What our psychological advisers have not been so quick to see or admit, however, is that "unloading on people" is the easiest way in the world to kill a relationship. If we regularly vent our hostility on another person, we can kill the relationship without really even trying to. We think we are being honest and ridding ourselves of repressed anger, but what we are actually doing is poisoning the relationship. The benefits that come from expressing our hostility are insignificant when compared to the damage our anger inflicts.

### Wounded by Words

As children we chanted, "Sticks and stones may break my bones, but words can never hurt me." Even as we said it, though, we knew it wasn't true. Words *can* hurt us—even more than sticks and stones. And the reason our angry words wreak such havoc on our relationships is that words have awesome power. When we hiss our bitterness or scream our rage, we are unleashing an explosive force on another person. "Those were just words," we rationalize after one of our verbal explosions. But when we say that, we are being naive and unobservant. Words can wound and even kill.

We need to recover the old Hebrew concept of words. The ancient Hebrews believed that a word had a life of its own, that it was like an arrow shot into the air, never again to be retrieved. That's why the psalmist could plead with God to deliver him from those who "aim their words like deadly arrows. They shoot from ambush at the innocent man; they shoot at him suddenly, without fear" (Psalm 64:3,4). The Old Testament Jew saw words as arrows that could inflict immeasurable damage upon another person. Words were deadly, and they could ambush and kill some unsuspecting soul.

If we could recover that concept, we would be much more hesitant to unleash our hostility on other people. We would realize that words have the power to wound and kill, and we would keep those dangerous arrows in their quiver where they belong. But sadly, that Hebrew concept is foreign to our minds today, and we go blithely on our way, firing verbal arrows into the air and then acting surprised when someone gets hurt.

I have seen the destruction of vented hostility, and so have you:

• In the middle of an argument over something silly, a husband shouts at his wife, "I wish I'd never married you!" She barely acknowledges the remark, and the spat continues without missing a beat. But the arrow went deep into her spirit, and she will carry the wound a long time. Of course he didn't mean it. He loves her, and he will eventually apologize for the remark. But the damage has been done.

• In a moment of frustration, a mother screams at her teenage daughter, "My life would've been so much easier if you'd never been born!" The daughter responds with venom of her own, and the tiff rages on until the daughter finally stalks off into her bedroom and slams the door. Once she has had time to cool off, the mother is sorry she said what she did. But it is entirely possible that her vented hostility has put a permanent scar on the relationship.

• After undergoing counseling for a multitude of emotional problems, the middle-aged man comes to the conclusion that most of his woes come from things his parents did to him in his childhood. The more he thinks about how his parents wronged him, the angrier he becomes. Finally he can't hold his anger any longer and places a call to his parents. Over the phone, he unloads his grief and tells his mother and father, "You have made my life miserable, and I'll never be able to forgive you for it." They express their regret and offer some lame excuses for their behavior. When he hangs up, the son feels both smug and cleansed. But it is likely that he has effectively killed any chance of reconciliation with his parents.

• In the midst of a parent-teacher conference at school, things get heated in a hurry. The parents believe the teacher is unfair; the teacher sees the parents as blind to the truth about their son. The more they talk, the more emotional and irrational the conversation becomes. Eventually the father stands and screams, "You are a complete idiot and have no business teaching in our schools! I'll see that you get exactly what you deserve!" The teacher tries to respond in a professional manner, but her quivering voice gives her away. She goes home from the encounter shaken and wondering if she should consider another profession. For several nights she has trouble sleeping.

Those four examples are not extraordinary; they are part and parcel of the contemporary scene. Some husbands regularly criticize their wives. Some mothers habitually scream at their daughters. Some sons consistently blame their parents for their problems. And some parents storm over to the schoolroom on a regular basis. Add to those examples all the other times hostility is vented, and you will see the enormity of the problem: the parents who curse the young umpire during a T-ball game, the friends who can't talk to each other five minutes without arguing, the bosses who lead by intimidation, the pastors who use the pulpit to browbeat people, and on and on.

Once those words of anger are spoken, once the arrows are flung into the air, they cannot be retrieved. The husband can assure his wife that his words were spoken in the heat of battle, and that he truly does love her, but the words have been launched and the damage has been done. The mother can tiptoe into her daughter's bedroom after their altercation and try to retract her "wish-you'd-never-been born" line, but the arrow has already gouged into the girl's heart. The middle-aged son may one day feel bad about criticizing his parents so harshly, but he will have a hard time mending the relationship. And should the parents of that boy decide to apologize for attacking the teacher, they can never remove the anguish she felt or the sleepless nights she endured.

The truth we must all remember before we utter a word in anger is this: Even if we can one day remove the arrow, we may never be able to heal the wound.

### Hedges Around Our Anger

We can prevent many relational wounds by putting some hedges around our anger. By "hedges" I mean protective promises we can make that will enable us to keep our temper in check. Three simple vows can put hedges around our anger and make our collisions more tender:

*First, I will never argue over trivial issues.* If we will build this one hedge, we will end about 99 percent of our arguing! If you think about it, there are precious few issues worth wrangling about. Some time, during one of your conflicts, stop and ask the question, "So what?"

You say the Yankees in the sixties were a better team than the Reds in the seventies. Your neighbor disagrees— vehemently! The conversation begins to smoke a little. And then you invoke the "so what?" solution. You ask that simple question and realize it really doesn't matter. Neither of you can prove your case, and even if you could, who cares? So you acknowledge that the Reds *were* a mighty powerful ball club and change the subject.

Or you and your husband start discussing the time your daughter should be home from her date. You suggest midnight; he thinks 11 is plenty late. Your discussion begins to rise in volume after awhile, and your ego starts to feel threatened. Soon you are caught in a full-blown power struggle, and the war of words escalates. Then you invoke the "so what?" solution. One hour either way is not going to affect your daughter's life very profoundly. So you tell him it really doesn't matter much to you, why don't we compromise at 11:30, and let's go down to the doughnut shop for a couple of apple fritters.

Or your co-worker is convinced that the apostle Paul wrote the book of Hebrews. You, on the other hand, are quite convinced that someone other than the great apostle wrote it. He cites his reasons, and you cite yours, and before you know it, you are in the midst of a full-scale theological war. He is questioning your scholarship, and you are just on the verge of questioning his conversion experience, when you remember the "so what?" solution. So what if Paul *did* write Hebrews? you ask. Does it really matter that much? Would it affect my commitment to the Bible? And then you compliment your fellow worker on his interest in Scripture and thank him for giving you a new perspective on Hebrews.

You see how it works? In the middle of any argument, you can employ the "so what?" solution and prevent much needless hassling. You'll eventually get conditioned to asking the "so what?" question and begin asking it even *before* a dispute arises.

*Second, I will never speak a word in anger when I am physically tired.* Physical exhaustion produces irritability and a critical attitude. So the second vow we can make to ourselves is that we will refrain from any expression of anger when we are tired.

I discovered several years ago that I most often lose my cool on Sunday evenings. After a long day of preaching, greeting worshipers, trying to stay atop the ministerial pedestal, and worrying about the things that didn't go well, I am always worn to a frazzle on Sunday nights. I began to notice that I was being critical of my wife and children in those times of tiredness, so I erected this hedge around my own life. Now, when I am tempted to speak a sarcastic word or launch into a verbal attack, I remember my vow and remain silent. At least on Sunday nights, if I can't say something nice, I'm not going to say anything at all.

Perhaps we have never thought of physical rest as a boon to our relationships, but when we are rested and relaxed we relate to people much easier. Rest ordinarily leads to companionship; exhaustion ordinarily leads to conflict. In fact, I have come to see that when I'm grumpy and short-tempered, it's time for me to ask if I'm tired and need a break from the routine.

In those times when we know we're tired but can't escape from the routine, we can at least remember this second hedge: Even though tired, I will not be tempted to speak even one word in anger.

*Third, I will never attack another person's "fragile spot."* We all have them, those "fragile spots" in our lives that are especially vulnerable. And it doesn't take a genius to figure out where those sensitive places are.

Think of the people you know best, and you can quickly determine their fragile spots. One person is sensitive about being overweight. Another thinks of herself as not too sharp intellectually. One is embarrassed because he is rapidly going bald. One hurts because she didn't make cheerleader last year. One is touchy because of his divorce. And one is humiliated because he has been fired from two jobs in recent months. We all have such sensitive areas in our lives, and when someone attacks those fragile spots, it is devastating.

Sadly, when we are angry we are prone to go right at those spots in the people we know. We attack them at their most vulnerable points to inflict as much pain on them as possible. Anger brings out the worst in us, so when we fire those verbal arrows we tend to aim straight for the heart. We zero in on our wife's weight problem, or our husband's lack of education, or our friend's financial difficulties—as if they themselves are not aware of their flaws. Eventually we will regret our insensitivity, but in the heat of a temper tantrum we are downright mean.

To prevent that from ever happening, we can build this third hedge and vow never to attack a person's fragile spot. We can declare this vulnerable area off-limits, and promise that we will never pour salt on an open wound.

Those three hedges can help us keep our anger under control. What they actually do is check our hostility *before* we vent it. They enable us to keep the arrows in the quiver where they can harm no one. But we need to erect those hedges *now*. We must make those three vows now and then remember them when our temper begins to flare and our voice begins to rise. I simply will not argue anymore over trivial matters. I simply will not speak an angry, critical word when I am tired. And I simply will not attack the fragile spot in a person's spirit.

If we will make those three vows and keep them, there is no telling how many relationships we will nurture—and how many potential heartaches we will prevent.

### Reactor or Responder?

In my high school physics class I learned a law that governs life in the physical world: For every action there is an opposite and equal reaction. Mr. Kohlmaier, my physics teacher, stressed that law repeatedly and made us commit it to memory. I may not know much physics today, but I still remember that fundamental law.

Since high school I have come to see that this law applies to human relationships as well. Generally, in human relationships, for every action there is an opposite and equal reaction. The Old Testament ethic that prescribed "an eye for an eye and a tooth for a tooth" expresses this law precisely. You gouge out my eye, and I have every right to gouge out yours. You knock out my tooth, and you'd better be ducking, because I'm going to try to knock out yours too.

I would hope that we don't literally gouge out eyes and knock out teeth as we relate to other people, but that old physical law still applies to how we usually act. If our husband is distant and sulky, we react with a distance and sulkiness of our own. If our children are surly with us, we react with a similar surliness. And if the people at the office are standoffish, we treat them with a matching apathy. Though we hate to admit it, others determine the quality of our relationships. We just return to them what they serve to us.

We are, to put it simply, reactors. And at no time is this more evident than when someone gets angry at us. Our normal reaction is to get angry in return. For every action there is an opposite and equal reaction, and this law nearly always becomes operative when anger is the initiating action. Anger breeds anger, which breeds more anger, and a whole cycle of anger is set in motion.

But we don't have to be reactors; we can be responders! We don't have to return anger for anger. We can choose to *respond* to people instead of reacting to them, and break that cycle of anger that can kill a relationship. When we choose to build those three hedges around our anger, we are choosing to respond instead of react. And say what you want about the homespun philosophy on my grandmother's plaque, at least it encourages responding over reacting.

Somebody in a relationship has to be strong enough to break the cycle of anger. It would be better, of course, if the cycle never got started in the first place. But once it is in motion, somebody has to become a responder. Somebody has to swallow some pride, deny self, and not return evil for evil. And if neither party is willing to do that, some serious wounds will inevitably be inflicted.

## Strange Words from Jesus

Only when we see it this way will the words of Jesus in the New Testament make sense to us. If we go to the New Testament for his counsel on anger and relationships, we will initially be amazed at what he says. On first reading, his advice will strike us as impractical and even impossible. But once we understand the reactor-responder option and once we realize that someone has to break the cycle of anger, his words will take on new meaning. Let us go to him with some personal, practical questions, and hear his words of response.

Question: What's the big deal about anger anyway? Doesn't everyone get mad from time to time? What's so wrong about blowing off some steam? Jesus' answer: "You have heard that it was said to the people long ago, 'Do not murder, and anyone who murders will be subject to judgment.' But I tell you that anyone who is angry with his brother will be subject to judgment" (Matthew 5:21,22).

I can't help but get angry when people treat me so shabbily. What am I supposed to do when somebody takes advantage of me, be a doormat? Jesus' answer: "You have heard that it was said 'Eye for eye, and tooth for tooth.' But I tell you, Do not resist an evil person. If someone strikes you on the right cheek, turn to him the other also. And if someone wants to sue you and take your tunic, let him have your cloak as well. If someone forces you to go one mile, go with him two miles. Give to the one who asks you, and do not turn away from the one who wants to borrow from you" (Matthew 5:38-42).

Boy, that just strikes me as so impossible! I think I'm a pretty loving person, but there are some people I just can't stand. I have a hard time not getting irritated at those people. What should I do about them? Jesus: "You have heard that it was said, 'Love your neighbor and hate your enemy.' But I tell you: Love your enemies and pray for those who persecute you, that you may be sons of your Father in heaven" (Matthew 5:43-45).

I have a hard enough time loving my neighbor, let alone my enemies! What can I do to get along better with people? Jesus: "Do not judge, or you too will be judged. For in the same way you judge others, you will be judged, and with the measure you use, it will be measured to you" (Matthew 7:1).

So I should just close my eyes to the faults of others and act like they're perfect? Just indiscriminately accept everybody? Jesus: "Why do you look at the speck of sawdust in your brother's eye and pay no attention to the plank in your own eye? How can you say to your brother, 'Let me take the speck out of your eye,' when all the time there is a plank in your own eye? You hypocrite, first take the plank out of your own eye, and then you will see clearly to remove the speck from your brother's eye" (Matthew 7:3-5).

Hey, you don't have to start calling me names! I just know that if I start relating to people this way, my friends and family are going to think I'm strange. Don't you see how weird this stuff is? No anger? Turning the other cheek? Loving your enemies? I would have to be a true nonconformist to try living like that. Jesus: "Enter through the narrow gate. For wide is the gate and broad is the road that leads to destruction, and many enter through it. But small is the gate and narrow the road that leads to life, and only a few find it" (Matthew 7:13,14).

Jesus' words do sound strange, don't they? They prescribe a style of relating to people that is foreign to even the finest among us. But they make a lot of sense if you filter them through the reactor-responder concept I've just mentioned. Jesus is telling us that we can *respond* to people instead of reacting to them. If someone strikes us on the cheek, we don't have to strike him back. If someone sees us as an enemy, we don't have to treat him as our enemy. If someone is critical of us, we don't have to be critical of him. In all of these examples, Jesus is underscoring the power we have to choose our response. He is telling us that the old law of physics doesn't have to hold sway in our relationships. We can choose to respond to people, and in the process either prevent or break the cycle of anger.

Even more convincing than his words, however, is his life. Jesus practiced what he preached. In the final days of his life, facing ridicule and death, he didn't react but responded. Standing before Pilate, he never got angry or descended to the level of his accusers. And when he died on the cross, he died forgiving his executioners, pardoning the penitent thief dying with him, and asking John to take care of his mother. No anger. No natural reaction to the cruelty he was experiencing. Nothing but an unbelievable love that has astounded people for 2000 years.

Jesus' response to the cross absolutely dumbfounded Simon Peter. You see, Peter was by nature a reactor. Come at him with a sword, as that soldier did in the Garden of Gethsemane, and he would whack your ear off with his own sword. He was a volatile, tempestuous man who was probably known for his outbursts of anger. Peter was ahead of his time; even in the first century, he was an expert at venting his hostility!

So how Jesus responded to the cross floored Peter, and he later described the scene this way: "When they hurled their insults at him, he did not retaliate; when he suffered, he made no threats. Instead, he entrusted himself to him who judges justly" (1 Peter 2:23). Peter was probably shaking his head in amazement when he wrote those words. Jesus didn't react, he responded. And Peter saw his response as an example for all of us: "To this you were called, because Christ suffered for you, leaving you an example, that you should follow in his steps" (1 Peter 2:21).

Just what does "following in his steps" mean? It means that we *respond* to people instead of reacting to them. It means that we don't have to return anger for anger. It means that we can *choose* how we will treat people. And it means that we have the power to break the cycle of anger that is ruining some of our relationships.

## Starting Over

The popular idea that venting our hostility is good and therapeutic needs to be challenged. As I mentioned in Chapter 1, the way we have always related to people needs to be challenged too. Occasionally we need to go back to square one and ask the simple question, Is this really true? Is it really true that unleashing our anger yields positive results? And is it really true that the way we've been treating people has led us to an abundance of loving relationships? The answer to both questions, I fear, is an emphatic *no*.

If the answer really is no, then the only sensible thing to do is to try something new—something like putting up the three hedges I've suggested and paying closer attention to the words and life of Jesus. If we do those things, it will be like starting over for us, a whole new philosophy and agenda for relationships. It will also put us on a narrow road with very few fellow travelers. The broad road will always be crowded with people who retaliate, criticize, and express their rage. Only a handful will embrace silence, turning the other cheek, and going the second mile. Without a doubt we will all continue to feel anger from time to time. Some things will happen to us that will make us fighting mad. What is yet to be seen, though, is how we will handle that anger and whether we react or respond to those frustrating people and circumstances.

When the next twinge of rage comes upon me, I hope I can remember what I've written here and respond accordingly. I'll do my best not to vent my hostility. And if I really start to get irritated? Well . . . I may just whisper a prayer and count slowly to ten.

> *We can make our collisions tender if we refrain from outbursts of anger that wound other people.*

# 4

## It's Okay to Be Ordinary

*Lurking beneath this infatuation with superstars is a devastating reality: We don't measure up, and neither do our friends and family! In a culture where only superstars are accorded status and worth, 99.9 percent of the people are destined to feel like failures.*

On Wednesday, May 19, 1982, Julian Nance Carsey disappeared. Jay Carsey, as he was called, was president of a college in Maryland, handsome, affluent, and married to a gorgeous socialite. To all who knew him he was living the American dream. But on that spring day in 1982 he chucked it all and vanished. A few days later his wife, Nancy, and several of his friends received brief notes in the mail indicating that he had left of his own free will. His note to his wife read:

I'm leaving because I know you can't. I am a physical and psychological disaster, I have no will to improve, and I don't want to drag you down with me. When you feel emotionally able, there is a tape in the right-hand drawer of my desk that you should listen to.

J

When she played the tape, she heard her husband calmly explain some things she needed to know about their financial situation. And that was it—Jay Carsey was gone, and nobody knew where he went.

His disappearance eventually attracted the attention of the media. The *Washington Post* did a story on the strange vanishing act of the college president, *People* magazine did a feature on the incident, and CBS news dispatched a reporter to the scene to investigate and report on Jay Carsey's disappearance. That reporter, Jonathan Coleman, would later write a book, *Exit the Rainmaker*, detailing the results of his investigation.

The question everyone wanted answered, of course, was *why*? Why would a successful college president with a beautiful wife, a 23-room mansion, and the world by the tail chuck it all and flee? It just didn't make sense to anyone, especially to those who knew him best and loved him most.

But, though they didn't know it, Jay Carsey had been miserable and disillusioned for years. His leaving was the result of many problems, problems he saw as basically unsolvable. But one factor seemed to stand above all others: He was tired of playing the role of superstar. All his life he had been placed on a pedestal. He was valedictorian of his high school class, a college president at the age of 29, a community leader who was wined and dined every weekend, and the husband of a woman bent on climbing even higher on the ladder of success. In short, he was "Wonder Boy," and he left primarily because he was sick of playing that role.

Jonathan Coleman would later describe Jay Carsey's predicament like this: "He realized that no matter how tired he was of the role that he—and everyone else—had become accustomed to his playing, it would be impossible—or so he thought—for him to change the equation, for people ever to see him as other than the president of the college, the high priest they had always been able to turn to with their problems."

## Life in a Superstar Culture

Jay Carsey eventually ended up in El Paso, Texas, where he changed his name and tried to become anonymous. For once in his life he wanted to be accepted for who he was, and not because he was a college president or rich or influential. He desperately wanted to be "ordinary," and his flight from his situation in Maryland was actually an attempt to find somebody who would accept him with no strings attached.

His story is extreme, and his method for finding acceptance was certainly misguided, but his impulse to be loved as an ordinary person is one I think we can all understand. Isn't that what we all crave—to be loved as we are? To know that we can be ordinary and still be accepted? To have somebody in our lives who will look beneath our accomplishments, successes, and image and love the "real us"?

I think we're all looking for that somebody who will love us that way. And I think our spouse, children, friends, and co-workers are looking for that somebody too. The key question is: Will we be that somebody for them?

If we decide that we *will* be, that we will accept our loved ones even though they are ordinary, we will definitely be going against the tide. Our culture today is a superstar culture that rewards those who have extra-special gifts. If you happen to be one of those superstars, you'll have no problem getting respect and applause in our society. But if you are ordinary, you'll have to scratch and claw for attention. We have gradually established a culture where esteem is earned by an easily discernible system of merit. In particular, we give honor to people who fall into any of the following four groups:

1. *The super-beautiful.* James Dobson in his book *Hide or Seek* calls beauty "the gold coin of human worth" in our society. If a person is born good-looking, he or she has a running start in the mad dash for acceptance. And since appearance is so crucial to earning our culture's "brownie points," we will pay fantastic sums of money to make ourselves more attractive. Men get hair transplants, women have makeovers and cosmetic surgery, and teenagers wouldn't be caught dead in jeans with the wrong label. Even kindergartners in our culture know how to hurl insults at the chubby boy with the big ears or to laugh at the little girl with the scarred face. It is just a fact of life in our society: Good looks cover a multitude of inadequacies, and bad looks cover a multitude of virtues.

2. *The super-smart.* Intelligence, Dobson asserts, is the "silver coin of human worth" in today's culture. Even if we are overweight or cursed with a large nose, we can still earn respect in our world if we can make straight A's

at school or be perceived as witty and clever. Businesses will pay large sums of money to people they deem sharp and creative.

3. *The super-talented.* Our culture also bequeaths adoration on anyone seen as possessing unusual talent in some area. The athlete who can hit a baseball 400 feet, or throw a football 70 yards on a line, or hit a golf ball with amazing finesse will never lack for attention. So too the person who can sing or dance or act with unique flair will be placed on a pedestal by most people in our culture. We typically reward these super-talented folks with both respect and hefty sums of money.

4. *The super-rich.* Even if someone in our culture doesn't have any of the three "coins of human worth" I've just mentioned, that person can still be admired if he or she is wealthy. Money buys more than possessions in our world; it also purchases honor and admiration. Every year certain magazines publish lists of the richest people in our country, and the goal of many of us is to someday be on that list ourselves. We are astute enough to know that if we could ever be on that list we would have not only the money we crave but also the acceptance that goes with it.

Anyone who falls into one of those four categories will be treasured in our society. And those lucky enough to have several of the "coins" will be idolized and almost deified—though they, like Jay Carsey, long to be accepted for who they are and not for what they do. The superstars will continue to make the headlines, and the rest of us will read about them with eager envy. We may never make "The Lifestyles of the Rich and

Famous" ourselves, but we love to tune in on those who do.

## The Plight of the Ugly Duckling

Lurking beneath this infatuation with superstars is a devastating reality: We don't measure up and neither do our friends and family! In a culture where only superstars are accorded status and worth, 99.9 percent of the people are destined to feel like failures.

Dobson in *Hide or Seek* describes our plight this way:

> Human worth in our society is carefully reserved for those who meet certain rigid specifications. The beautiful people are born with it; those who are highly intelligent are likely to find approval; superstar athletes are usually respected. But no one is considered valuable just because he *is*! Social acceptance is awarded rather carefully, making certain to exclude those who are unqualified.

Only a small fraction of the population is "qualified," so the rest of us spend our lives feeling like the ugly duckling. We go through life with an inferiority complex because we're not superstars. In spite of our finest efforts, we still don't look like Tom Cruise or Kim Basinger. In spite of hours of study, we still can't crack the dean's list. In spite of years of dedication to our craft, we still can't hit a baseball like Jose Canseco or sing like Barbra Streisand. And in spite of a whole lifetime of hard work, we still don't have the money of the Rockefellers or the Hunts. Most of us are stuck in "ordinariness," and we're doing our best to cope with being "average."

## Loving Ordinary People

So this is our world. We adore superstars, and all of us would like to attain that status, but only a few of us ever will. Painful as it will be to do it, let's look at what this truth means for our personal relationships. I hate to "burst your bubble" and destroy your fantasy, but what this truth means is:

• It is entirely possible, ladies, that your husband will never be the handsome, debonair gentleman you would like him to be. He may never have the looks of Robert Redford or the charm of Sean Connery. He may, in fact, be rather paunchy in appearance and rather crabby in attitude.

• It is entirely possible, men, that your wife will never be the sexy, sophisticated woman you hoped she would be. She may never live up to your fantasy, and you will have to adjust to life with a woman who looks frumpy in the morning and acts grumpy more than she should.

• It is entirely possible, parents, that your son will never make it to the big leagues. I know he just pitched a shutout in the Little League all-star game, but he just might discover that the competition gets pretty fierce as he gets older, and not be able to measure up. And then you will have to adjust to an ordinary son and not a superstar-athlete son.

• It is also entirely possible, parents, that your daughter will never make it to Hollywood. I know she starred in the kindergarten play last year and everyone raved about her performance, but she might get interested in boys somewhere along the way and decide that drama is not her thing after all. And then you'll have to accept her as an ordinary daughter and not a future starlet.

• It is entirely possible, parishioners, that your preacher will never hold you spellbound with his sermons. "Dynamic" he may never be. In fact, he just might turn out to be so ordinary that you can't depend on him to do everything the church needs done. And then you'll have to carry the load with him.

• And it is entirely possible, friends, that your friends won't turn out to be anything very special. They'll get depressed occasionally, gossip from time to time, have money troubles, and show other telltale signs of being terribly human. And then you'll have to decide whether you want to love them anyway or go in search of some perfect friends.

Depressing, isn't it? In a superstar culture, we're stuck with ordinary people! I'm convinced that one of the reasons our collisions are so abrasive is that we've never accepted that fact. We continue to expect superstar performances out of ordinary people, and we're disappointed when they don't meet our expectations. And *they*, in turn, are disappointed because they *know* they're not meeting our expectations. It is terribly frustrating to try to relate to someone who won't accept you if you're "average." But that is precisely the bind we put people in when we demand that they be superstars.

### Examining Our Expectations

Fifteen years ago I was given the unique opportunity of beginning a church from scratch. Since I was going to be able to build the church from the ground up, without any old ideologies to undo or outdated traditions to uphold, I determined that our church would be different. I envisioned us as "the church of tomorrow," on the cutting edge of what God wanted to do in the world.

Since the church was located near NASA in Houston with a potential parish of educated, well-to-do people, I envisioned us as a biblically literate, theologically trained group who would think new thoughts and share deep insights. I saw us forming a unique community of love and fellowship. I fantasized families hurrying to church each Sunday, anxious to learn new nuggets of truth from their brilliant young pastor. I saw the church nurturing those families and protecting them from the demons of our society. I pictured the church as a place of emotional wholeness, where people could be healed from the wounds of a hectic and violent society. I envisioned non-Christians hearing about this "different kind of church" and being drawn into our fellowship. In short, I expected the people I would be pastoring to be innovative, intellectually keen, grounded in theology, excited about our adventure, emotionally fit, and contagious in their witness—spiritual superstars, in other words.

And so we began. Built a new building. Elected leaders. Established a budget. Set some priorities. Began having worship and Bible study every week. And, most importantly, started to get acquainted with one another.

Frankly, getting acquainted with one another proved to be one of the most helpfully disillusioning experiences I had ever had. For what I learned as we became acquainted was that these people, much to my dismay and benefit, were terribly ordinary. Some of them barely knew the books of the Bible. Some of them were going through depression. Some were having family problems. Some wanted to argue over every comma in our bylaws. Once, we debated (argued?) for an hour over whether to order 100 folding chairs or 120 folding chairs. Those outside our church looked at our "unique" fellowship—and yawned. My vision of a church of superstar saints was quickly (and painfully!) replaced by a new vision: I realized I was in the midst of ordinary people with ordinary problems.

Those people, I'm sure, were going through the same process in their thinking about me. They thought they had hired a superstar preacher; what they got was an ordinary guy who sometimes hit the homiletical target and sometimes missed by a mile. They thought they were getting an updated version of the apostle Paul; what they got was an updated version of me—with all my doubts and flaws and peculiarities.

But, amazingly, I'm still at that church. We somehow made the mental shift from expecting superstardom to accepting ordinariness, and we have learned to love each other. These days when I stand to preach I aim my message at ordinary folks. Perhaps someplace else the Word is delivered to the superstars, but at our place we're all hurting, all doubting, all struggling, and all trying to learn the fundamentals of the Christian faith. If there is a superstar among us, she has yet to raise her super-beautiful, super-smart, super-talented, or super-rich head.

And that shift from expecting people to be superstars to accepting them as ordinary is the one we need to make with all of the people in our lives. You see, it really is okay for them to be ordinary. We can learn to love our wife, husband, children, parents, and friends even though they're not superstars. Learning to love that way is one of the key secrets of the tender collision.

## Rummaging in the Basement

Easier said than done, however. As with all of the ideas in this book, it is much easier to know we *ought* to love unconditionally than it is to actually do it. But the place to begin as we try to learn unconditional love is to ask ourselves: Why do I love conditionally in the first place? Why do I attach so many strings to my relationships? What prompts me to withhold acceptance from the ordinary people in my life?

If we will ask those kinds of questions, we will eventually come up with some answers—though we probably won't like the answers we get. The chances are good that if we go rummaging around in the basement of our motives and desires, we will uncover some dirty junk that we would just as soon not see. Go rummaging around deep in your soul for the answer to "Why do I put so much pressure on people to perform?" and you will likely be confronted by three old, junky words.

The first word you will stumble upon is "seduction." When we value only the superstars, we have fallen into step with our culture and have been seduced into a style of relating to people that leads to judgmental misery. One Bible verse that should be memorized by everyone in our society is 1 Samuel 16:7: "Man looks on the outward appearance, but the Lord looks at the heart." That verse relates to the choosing of David as King of Israel. Remember the story? David's brothers were bigger, stronger, more experienced. They were, to all human observers, much better "king material" than the little shepherd boy. But God had different standards. He didn't look on the outward appearance—he looked at the heart.

And so should we! All those external criteria we have established have no eternal significance at all. Beauty vanishes in time. Intelligence is useless unless used for good ends. Talent fades with the years. And money, as Jesus reminds us, is easy prey for moths, rust, and thieves. When we refuse to love our spouse or children because they're not "super-something," we've been seduced by the standards of men and forsaken the standard of God.

The second word we will probably uncover down there in the basement is "compensation." Most of our judgment of others is, quite simply, compensation for our own inadequacies. As Jesus put it in the Sermon on the Mount, "Do not judge, or you too will be judged" (Matthew 7:1). In judging others, we reveal our own flaws.

How many fathers, for example, put undue pressure on their children to succeed at sports because they themselves were never as good at sports as they wanted to be? They want their children to be superstar athletes to compensate for their own lack of ability. And how many mothers put pressure on their daughters to be pretty and popular because they themselves were not as pretty and popular as they wanted to be back in their youth? You see how it works? In judging others we always judge ourselves. We always reveal those inadequacies in our lives that we're trying to compensate for.

The third word we'll find down in that junky basement is "reflection." One friend of Jay Carsey's, commenting on his disappearance, said, "The more public a figure you are, the more power that you wield, the more you wonder if people like you for you, or if they like you because when they're around you *they* are in the spotlight." Isn't it true that we want our family and friends to be superstars because that reflects so well on *us*? Because it puts *us* in the spotlight?

We want our husband to be the most handsome, personable man at the party because it reflects so favorably on us. We want our children to be great successes because their success reflects so well on us. We want our friends to be famous and wealthy because their fame and wealth reflects kindly on us. It all goes back to that selfish self that is the main deterrent to loving relationships. That self desperately wants to look good, and it loves to bask in the reflection of superstar acquaintances.

Conditional, "I-will-accept-you-if-you-measure-up" relationships are built on seduction, compensation, and reflection. If we can ever get that trash out of the basement of our souls, we can begin to accept people with no strings attached. Once we decide to accept God's standard instead of culture's, once we quit feeling so inferior over our failures, and once we quit relying on other people's accomplishments for our self-worth, we can better accept people as they are.

Junky souls always produce criticism; clean souls invariably lead to acceptance.

### Parents Beware!

He came to the game with his videocamera and a tripod, eager to capture his daughter on film. And it was obvious as the game began that she was the star of her team—over six feet tall, good moves, nice jump shot. But it also became obvious that she was "off" this particular night. Her shots were not falling, and she seemed to be a step slow on defense.

As the game progressed and she continued to struggle, her father became more and more agitated. He started screaming instructions to her from the stands, and the more the girl struggled the louder he screamed. By the second half he was out of control. His face was red, his voice was raspy, and his instruction had degenerated into verbal abuse. His behavior was embarrassing—especially, I'm sure, to his daughter!

What happened at that basketball game? Something, tragically, that happens frequently in our culture: a parent getting mad because his offspring looks ordinary. If that screaming session at the basketball game was an isolated incident, we could dismiss it and assume the father was just having a bad day. But that incident represents a common parental attitude in our culture: If you can't be a superstar, child, I'll be very disappointed in you and might even throw a fit.

Of course most of us are more subtle than the father at the basketball game. We don't shout our conditional acceptance from the grandstands, but we communicate it nonetheless—through facial expressions, voice inflections, and private words of disappointment and anger. And we can be sure that if our love for our children is conditional, they *will* know it. They don't have to be geniuses to perceive that high achievement is the currency that buys our acceptance.

Of all the groups that most need the message of this chapter, parents top the list. Somehow, some way, we have to let our children know that we love them unconditionally. Even if our daughter can't hit the backboard one night, she needs to know that our acceptance is not affected by how many points she scores. Even if she doesn't make straight A's, or get elected cheerleader, or earn a college scholarship, she needs to know that she is loved with no strings attached. She needs a mother and father who will delight in her for who she is, and not for what she has accomplished.

Even as I write this, I know how hard this is to do. Those of us who are parents are walking a precarious tightrope. We want to challenge our children to reach their full potential. We want them to succeed. We want them to be popular, to have a good life, to earn the acceptance of others. All good parents have those desires for their offspring.

But take those natural parental desires and mix in seduction, compensation, and reflection, and you suddenly have a deadly concoction. What started as "wanting them to reach their full potential" inadvertently and unconsciously becomes "not accepting them if they don't measure up." Let that normal parental wish for successful children become tinged with seduction ("This is the way everybody measures success"), compensation ("I want him to succeed where I failed"), and reflection ("Her success shows what a fine person and parent I am"), and what you end up with is a severe case of conditional love.

I need to underscore that this process happens inadvertently and unconsciously. No parent consciously decides to withhold love from a child or to dangle the carrot of acceptance before a child's eyes. But withholding love and dangling that carrot happen all the time. Good Christian parents frequently communicate conditional love to their children without even intending to. They just want their children to do well in life. They just yield to the tempting sins of seduction, compensation, and reflection. And, as a result, their children spend their lives straining and struggling not to appear ordinary.

## The Power of One

Once we are aware of our tendency to love people conditionally, we can begin to change. We can face up to seduction, compensation, and reflection, acknowledge them as problems, and then start battling them. Once we do, we will make an amazing discovery. We will discover that unconditional love unleashes unbelievable power. Our husband, wife, children, friends, or whoever is the recipient of our acceptance will be nurtured and sustained as never before. Unconditional love is so powerful that it takes only one such relationship to transform a person's life. If a person has one other person who will love him unconditionally, he will be able to weather many an emotional storm and feel surprisingly secure in an incredibly insecure society.

This unbelievable power of acceptance was one of the secrets of Jesus' life and one of the primary reasons people were changed in his presence. The people he called as his disciples, if you think about it, were not superstars. They were ordinary fisherman, tax collectors, husbands, and fathers, and every one a sinner. But Jesus called them to him, loved them as they were, and assured them that nothing in all of creation could separate them from his love. Imagine what it would do for your confidence to be loved unconditionally by someone like Jesus!

And, true to his word, he *did* love them unreservedly. Even after they all forsook him at the cross, he came back after the resurrection to remind them again of his undying love for them. They had clearly displayed that they were ordinary. They had denied him, run from the Roman authorities, doubted his resurrection, and gone into hiding like scared children in a thunderstorm. What they deserved was ridicule and condemnation; what they got was unqualified acceptance. Jesus appeared to them, reassured them of his love, and called them again to be his people in the world.

He knew what you and I need to know: *He knew the awesome power of a love that arrives with no strings attached.* Peter, James, John, Andrew, and all the rest were just ordinary men. No superstar saint among them. No super-beautiful, super-smart, super-talented, or super-rich man in the bunch. But if they knew they were loved unconditionally by just one person, they could do extra-ordinary things. They could live with confidence and joy. Knowing that their place was secure in just *one* heart, they could take whatever life threw at them.

And that, you see, is the gift we can give our loved ones. We can be that one person for them. We can love them just because they *are*, and not because they *do*. In a world where they have to scratch and claw for approval, we can offer them approval even if they're ordinary.

If we will do that for them, if we will buck the tide and chuck culture's merit system, we will give them the finest gift that any person can bestow upon another. The Bible calls that gift "grace," and grace will do more for a person than all the beauty, intelligence, talent, or money in the world.

> *We can make our collisions tender if we quit expecting people to be superstars and give them permission to be ordinary.*

# 5

# Square Pegs and Round Holes

*It is not within our power to change people. If they don't change themselves, change will never take place. We can love people, pray for them, offer suggestions, and even confront them, but we cannot change them. The more we try to change people, the worse our relationships will become.*

*H*e *was definitely a caterpillar*, but I could see the butterfly he could become. So I took him on as a "project." True, his family background was awful and he had no money, no job, no plans. True, he had failed miserably in the Army and had a long history of other failures. And true, most people saw him as hopeless, as someone who never would acquire any of the "coins of human worth" we deem so important. But I took him on anyway.

I first found him a job; he lost it in a matter of months. I found him an apartment; he was evicted for non-payment in short order. I loaned him some money; he squandered it on nonessentials. I let him move in with me and my family; he wrecked our car and quickly wore out his welcome. After just a few months he was back on the streets, and I was forced to declare my reclamation project a colossal failure.

But undaunted, I pressed on and found another "project"—this time a young woman who was homeless, penniless, and friendless. Again I found her a job. Again I gave her money. Again I let her move in with us for several months. And again, the project ended in failure. She moved out, and, despite my best efforts, was still a lonely wanderer.

I would like to think that my attempts to help those two people were not totally in vain. Maybe I did more for them than I realize. Maybe I had a bigger impact on them than I know. But the sad truth is that, in both instances, the caterpillars I tried to change never emerged into butterflies. Though I envisioned both of them as "round hole" people, they were quite content at being "square pegs." And nothing I did could force them into a different shape.

## The Limits of Personal Power

I don't regret getting involved with them, however. They needed help, and I thought I could help them. Besides, as a Christian, I know that God has called me to be a "creative change agent" in the world. The Bible tells me to be "the salt of the earth," "the light of the world," "an ambassador for Christ," and a "witness." To follow

Christ means that we work for change in the world and in the lives of the people around us.

But my relationship with those two needy people *did* remind me of something I am prone to forget: I don't have the power to change anyone. At best, I can provide the atmosphere where people can choose to change. But change is an "inside job." It starts from *within* a person, and, if it doesn't start there, change will never take place in that life. You see, I had a vision for both of those people; unfortunately, neither of them shared that vision. I saw them as potential butterflies; they saw themselves as caterpillars and were quite content being what they were.

In the last chapter we looked at our desire to be surrounded by superstars. A natural corollary to that desire is the desire to change people into what we think they should be. Since we readily see the changes that people need to make, and since as Christians we're called to be "change agents," we feel it our duty to launch improvement campaigns for others. We see it as our task to improve our husband's laziness, or to make our wife lose weight, or to motivate our friend to be more truthful. Though we would never couch it in these terms, we see it as our calling to help ordinary people move toward superstar status.

But when we launch these improvement campaigns on behalf of these needy folks we usually find, much to our surprise, that they don't like our agenda. In fact, we find that our collisions with these people become anything but tender. All we want to do is help them reach their full potential. All we desire is that they be happy. But what we receive in return is resentment. People who feel pressure to change *from outside* inevitably get irritated at the person trying to initiate the change. And the sooner we realize this, the more tender our relationships can become.

## The Ingredients of Change

Perhaps we should begin with a refresher course in the process of change. Every change in our lives involves four ingredients, and if any of these four is missing, lasting change cannot take place. The four ingredients of change are 1) Problem, 2) Awareness, 3) Initiative, and 4) Review. Just remember the acronym P-A-I-R, and that will remind you of the four ingredients of change.

First, change occurs because there is a *problem*. The marriage has grown stale, the kids are getting out of hand, our weight has skyrocketed, the bills are more than the monthly paycheck, our depression has grown darker, or the job has become unbearable. There is a *problem* lurking in our lives, and this problem signals the beginning of change.

The New Testament talks about the law of sowing and reaping. "A man reaps what he sows," it says (see Galatians 6:7). That is a wonderful, God-ordained law that invites us to look at our lives and to make necessary changes. If we are reaping misery, depression, or constant hassle in our relationships, we can begin to sow some new seed that will eventually produce a better crop. The law of sowing and reaping is an invitation to survey our crop right now to see what we're reaping. And if we're not happy with what we see, we can begin sowing something different. I hope this book itself can be a tool to help you put some new seed in your life.

But the point is that change ordinarily begins with a problem. Something is "broken" and needs to be fixed.

From this vantage point problems are not negative but positive. They nudge us to change.

Second, there is an *awareness* of the problem. Just having a problem is not sufficient to motivate us. We have to become acutely *aware* of the problem. All sorts of people have problems and never change. Only people who are aware of their problems and bothered by them are motivated to act.

The woman who has a malignancy, we would all agree, has a serious problem. But she won't address that problem until her cancer is diagnosed and she becomes aware of it. So too can we have some severe problems— poor marriages, undisciplined children, a lack of intimacy with anyone—but something has to happen to make us aware of those problems if we're ever going to change.

We all have the knack for "selective consciousness." That means we can tune out the things we find unpleasant. We just play "ostrich in the sand" and refuse to let those ugly things enter our minds. Problems abound, but the ostrich obstinately keeps his eyes diverted. The second ingredient of change—awareness—usually comes because some painful circumstance won't allow us to divert our eyes.

Third, there is *initiative*. Once we become aware of the problem, we then have to decide if we will take the initiative to address it. If we do, we will formulate a plan of attack: how we will improve the marriage, how we will control the kids, which diet we will begin to shrink our waistline, what we can do to increase our income, how we can lift the cloud of depression, or what we can do to survive our job misery.

This third ingredient in the change process is the crucial one. Having a problem and being aware of that problem don't in themselves mean that a person will change. The first two steps are just preparation for this key third step: We take some initiative and *do* something to change. Initiative is the fuel that actually gets the rocket of transformation off the launching pad.

Fourth, there is *review*. This is the evaluation phase of the change process. We examine our action plan and decide if change is taking place. The questions we ask ourselves in this review step are often unconscious but vital: Is the marriage getting better because of my efforts? Are my children becoming more disciplined? Have I lost weight on this diet? Have I generated enough money to pay the bills this month? Is the cloud of depression starting to lift? Am I finding more job satisfaction than before?

This fourth ingredient in the change process tells us whether or not our efforts are paying off. If we decide they are, we will continue to change. If we decide they are not, we will likely scrap the transformation project and return to our old habits.

Those four steps are part of any lasting change that will take place in our lives. First, we have a problem. Second, something happens to make us acutely aware of that problem. Third, we initiate some action that will alleviate the problem. And fourth, we review our action to see if the desired change is happening.

### The Frustration of Trying to Change People

Once we understand the change process, we can easily see why our efforts to change people are so frustrating.

The first step we can negotiate with no trouble at all. Goodness knows, there are plenty of problems in our world! If problems are indeed the seedbed for change, there are a lot of changes that need to take place.

And we are even more proficient at step two—being aware of those problems. As Jesus points out in the Sermon on the Mount, we are expert at seeing the speck in our brother's eye but blind to the plank that is in our own eye. We have no trouble seeing all the flaws in our husband, wife, kids, and friends; we are not so adept, however, at noticing the areas in our own lives that need to be changed. And of course we are good at pointing out to our friends and loved ones the changes they need to make. If they cannot see them for themselves, we feel that it is our responsibility to make them aware of their shortcomings.

So far, so good. There are plenty of problems in people's lives. We can see those problems clearly and can communicate our findings to those people so they can change. So far the change process is moving along on well-oiled wheels.

It is at step three, however, that the whole process comes to a screeching halt. Though there are problems with other people and though we can make them aware of those problems, we cannot take the initiative for them to address those problems. Initiative must be generated *inside* a person. If it is not, we cannot manufacture it for them.

That is why trying to change people so often ends in frustration. We can see the problem in their lives, but we cannot bestow upon them the willingness to change. That is why my efforts with my two "projects" ended in failure. They both had problems. I could see those problems clearly (and so could they). But I couldn't provide enough initiative from the outside to effect any lasting change. Unless from *within* them there was the motivation to get up and go to work, or balance their checkbook, or pay their bills, or get along with their boss, all my finest efforts at helping them were doomed to failure.

And the fourth step—review—is beyond our power too. We simply cannot evaluate for people how their lives are going. That too is an *inner* activity that each person must do for himself.

So now you see our plight. We can take people through the first two steps of the change process, but steps three and four are beyond our power. We can't take initiative for people, and we can't evaluate their lives for them. We're stuck, in other words, in a baffling predicament. We have the power to see the problems of other people, but we don't have the power to solve them.

## A Blessing in Disguise?

Before we curse our fate and bemoan our pitiful lack of power, there is one compensating truth we need to consider. That truth is that if we had the power to change people, we would always make them in our own image. If we had the power to turn caterpillars into butterflies, the spots on their wings would be identical to ours.

What I had in mind for my two "projects" was that they would live like I do. To be successful human beings they needed a heavy dose of my beliefs, my habits, my style of relating to people, my personality. Though we never come out and say it, the change we envision for others would enable them to be more like *us*. After all, though we may not be perfect, we do "have it together" more than the people we're trying to help.

But on our more honest days we would probably admit that molding people into our image might not be ideal. It just might be okay for my kids to be different than I am. It just might be okay for my wife to march to a different drummer than I do. And it just might be okay if there is diversity in the world, if some people's idea of a successful life doesn't exactly match mine.

One time I wrote a little poem that struggled with this idea. I share it with you now with the hope that it will remind you that our differences with people might be a blessing in disguise.

### IF EVERYBODY WAS JUST LIKE ME

If everybody was just like me...
   The world would surely be a better place to be.
      There would be no murder, for I'm not violent.
      No stealing, for I'm not a thief.
      No adultery, for I'm happily wed.
      No atheism, for I believe in God.
      No ignorance, for I've been to school.
If only the world was more like me...
   Surely it would be a better place to be.

Or would it?
   For if everybody was just like me...
      There would be no merry-go-rounds, for I get dizzy.
      No clowns, for I'm self-conscious.
      No doctors, for I hate blood.
      No painters, for I'm color blind.
      No mechanics, for I can't fix anything.
      No elevator operators, for I'm claustrophobic.
      No home run kings, for I can't hit a curve.
      No balloon riders, for I'm afraid of heights.

> Come to think of it,
> If the world was just like me...
> It would be an awfully boring place to be!

## Dead-End Streets

But still we try to change people, to make them into what we think they should be. And without a doubt people do need to change! It's obvious: Our husband is lazy and lets the yard go to pot; our wife is not as sexy as she should be and needs to take sensuality lessons; our daughter is too flighty and overly smitten with boys; our parents are undereducated and need to improve their grammar. It's just very obvious to any discerning person that the people in our lives are terribly ordinary and definitely need to change.

The techniques we typically use to effect those changes often lead to disaster, though. In trying to implement those obviously needed changes in the lives of our friends and family, we resort to some age-old methods that are guaranteed to hurt our relationships.

"The Halo Technique," for example, always engenders resentment. This technique involves elevating self and deprecating the other person. It says things like this: "Listen, I lost 40 pounds last year. Why can't you?" Guaranteed, you see, to make someone feel warm and toasty toward us! Or: "All I'm asking is that you be as responsible as I am." Or: "Son, I worked nights and went to school full-time when I was your age. You need to get with the program and stop sleeping until noon every day." Somehow we have gotten the idea that putting on a halo and offering ourself as a model of perfection will prompt people to change. It won't.

Then there's "The Doghouse Technique." This technique puts people in the doghouse by informing them that we're offended by something they've done. Those who have mastered this technique can put people in the doghouse just by looking at them a certain way or by uttering a few well-chosen remarks. However we choose to communicate it, we let it be known that we are offended and that some reparation needs to be made if that person is to get back in our good graces. Even hasty reflection will reveal why this technique has been so popular through the years: If somebody else is in the doghouse, it assures us that we're not the dog! "The Doghouse Technique" turns out to be a first cousin, then, to "The Halo Technique."

Or we try "The Mirror Technique." We reflect back to people exactly what they give us. We try to show them how bad they are by acting equally bad toward them. You get sulky and silent with me, and I'll get sulky and silent with you. You get angry with me, and I'll get angry with you. You run around on me, and I'll run around on you. "The Mirror Technique" is but a modern version of the "eye-for-an-eye" and "tooth-for-a-tooth" ethic of the Old Testament. And it's built upon the faulty assumption that two wrongs will somehow help a person see what is right.

Or we try "The Tantrum Technique." This has been one of the most popular techniques for getting people to change for centuries. When all else fails, erupt into hostility. Raise your voice. Call them bad names. Shame them. Throw a first-class tantrum, and surely people will humble themselves, beg your forgiveness, and make immediate changes, right? Wrong! People typically will respond with a tantrum of their own, and the only change that takes place is the negative one that occurs in your relationship with that person.

Or perhaps we resort to "The Public Flogging Technique." This is a favorite of married couples. The purpose of this technique is to effect change by embarrassing someone publicly. "The Public Flogging Technique" relies upon shame for its effectiveness. Shame someone in public, it assumes, and that person will be obliged to change. And, like "The Doghouse Technique," it also enables the flogger to feel superior and self-righteous.

Whenever we employ those techniques, we are dipping into an old bag of tricks. Humans have been trying those techniques on each other ever since Eden. And they never have worked! But we don't know what else to do, so we put on the halo, banish people to the doghouse, reflect their badness back to them, throw a screaming fit, or shame them in public. Even if we become certified experts in some of those old techniques, though, people will not change because of them. Those old techniques are dead-end streets on the roadmap that leads to authentic change.

### The Magic of Freedom

The question is, then, how do we implement change in these people with whom we must live? How do we help "square pegs" fit into "round holes"?

The answer is: We don't. It is not within our power to change people. If they don't change themselves, change will never take place. We can love people, pray for them, offer suggestions, and even confront them. But we cannot change them. The more we try to change people, the worse our relationships will become. There is no technique we can use that has the power to transform another person.

The best way to help people change, ironically, is to give them freedom. I know that sounds silly. If we give people freedom, won't they abuse it? Won't they stay stuck where they are and never become what they should become? Well, possibly. But granting freedom has had a much higher success rate than any of the other techniques we usually try. And the reason freedom is more effective is because it puts the initiative where it must be—*within* the other person.

Of course there is risk involved when we let go of the strings and give someone personal sovereignty. That person surely might abuse his liberty and make a mess of his life. But, you see, it is *his* life. And while we can love, pray, suggest, and confront, we cannot live his life for him. Even if he falls flat on his face, that failure in itself may be what it takes to set the change process into motion. As difficult as it is for us to believe it, there is magic in freedom.

Just in case you need further convincing, I want you to think for a moment about your relationship with God. The Bible makes it very clear that God wants us to change—that as a loving Father he longs for us to become all that he created us to be. The passionate desire of God is that we all change and become conformed to the image of Jesus Christ.

Now let me ask you: How does he prompt us to change? Does he bully us? Badger us? Scream at us? No, he gives us freedom! One of the most common complaints registered against God is that he is too "low-key," that he doesn't come out in the open enough to tell us what we need to do. God seems so "hidden" that people get upset at his lack of initiative. But I think that is part of his plan!

He is intentionally staying in the background because he knows that true change can only occur in an atmosphere of freedom. If he coerced us, made decisions for us, and put constant pressure on us, we might change for awhile, but the transformation would be temporary. It would last only as long as the coercion lasted.

I think God knows that since freedom always surrounds authentic change, the one thing we all need from him is that very freedom. We might not like it. We might wish he would be more aggressive. We might wish he would remove from us the responsibility of taking the initiative to change. But he won't. And he won't because he really desires that we change—from the inside out.

If we take our cue from God, then, we too will give that gift of freedom to the people we know and love. If an all-knowing and all-powerful God can give people freedom, surely we ignorant and powerless humans should learn to do the same.

I must, however, offer two disclaimers. This concept of giving people their freedom is true, with two exceptions. When people are either too young or too emotionally distraught to handle freedom, we should not give it to them. Obviously, what I am writing here does not apply to little children who are not mature enough to handle freedom. Little children must be taught, guided, and disciplined, so that by the time they are teenagers they know how to handle freedom and can become responsible for their lives.

Some emotionally distraught adults can revert to a childlike state too, and not be able to handle freedom responsibly. If, for example, our teenager is on drugs, that teenager is out of control, and his freedom needs to be removed. Or if a friend calls and hints at suicide, that friend is so emotionally disturbed that granting her freedom would be a serious mistake. Or if we know our spouse is having an affair, that spouse needs to be confronted and told that such dishonesty will not be tolerated. To say in any of those extreme situations "They're free to do whatever they wish" is a denial of love for those people.

But those are drastic cases. The general rule still holds for the vast majority of the relational situations we will encounter: Freedom is the forerunner of change. To deny freedom is to keep a person in bondage to old ways. To bestow freedom is to give a person opportunity to change.

### The Critical Question

Jesus once asked a bizarre-sounding question that underscores the importance of personal initiative in the change process. He was passing through Jerusalem when he encountered an invalid lying by the Pool of Bethesda (see John 5:1-15). John tells us the man had been an invalid for 38 years, and then he writes, "When Jesus saw him lying there and learned that he had been in this condition for a long time, he asked him, 'Do you want to get well?'"

What a question! It seems ridiculous, doesn't it? Someone who has been an invalid for 38 years would naturally want to be healed, wouldn't he? What would prompt Jesus to ask such a question?

I think what Jesus was asking was, "Do you really want to change?" You see, Jesus knew he had the power to heal the man's physical ailment. But he also knew that no permanent change would take place unless the man was willing to take some personal initiative. Was he ready, after 38 years as a handicapped person, to assume the responsibility of being a normal person? Was he willing to earn a living, relate in a new way to the people around him, assume his place in his family, and face up to his new moral and spiritual obligations? Was he really desiring change? Or did he just want his body healed?

Then, as if to really test the man, Jesus said to him, "Get up! Pick up your mat and walk." In other words, Jesus left the ball in his court. If you'll take the initiative to get up, pick up your mat, and walk, I can do something for you. If you won't take that initiative, I can't help you.

That is true for all people and is the prime truth I've been trying to help you see in this chapter. The crucial question is "Do you want to get well?" Our response to the people around us will be determined by how they answer that question.

If the honest answer is no, we are doomed to frustration if we try to change those people. We can still love them, pray for them, and give them freedom, but we cannot change them. And if we resort to badgering and bickering with them over those changes, we will only harm the relationship.

But if the honest answer is yes, then we can really make a difference in the lives of those people. We can encourage them in a multitude of ways and applaud them when the change starts taking place. Once *they* decide to get up, take up their mat, and walk, we can be an agent of healing in their lives.

## The Bad News and the Good News

We've all heard more than our share of those "good news-bad news" jokes. There is no shortage of such jokes making the rounds in our society. As I come to the end of this chapter, I have some good news and some bad news for you. Let me give you the bad news first. The bad news is that you don't have the power to change anyone. No matter how smart you might be or how proficient you've become at the techniques of manipulation, you can't change even one person.

The good news is that, though you think you want that power, you're better off without it. If we had the power to effect change in others, we would spend all our time making clones of ourselves. We would be constantly intruding into the lives of other people, demanding that they change, demanding that they act more like us. Once we realize we're not in the business of changing others, we can relax and begin to ponder the plank that is in our own eye. Frankly, we have all we can handle in just trying to change ourselves.

And that's no joke.

---

*We can make our collisions tender if we quit trying to change people and give them the freedom to be different from us.*

# 6

# *The People of the Late Afternoon*

*If we see ourselves as "people of the late afternoon,"
our whole perspective will be different. If we see
ourselves as the guy who showed up at quitting time
and got the full day's pay, we will be filled with
celebration.*

N*ot long ago* I pulled into a local service station to get
gas for my minivan. The station was "self-serve,"
so I put the nozzle in my gas tank, flipped the lever
on the pump to "on," and waited for the gas to start
pouring into my tank. Nothing happened, so I flipped
the lever again, reread the instructions on the top of the
pump, and waited. Still no action.

Suddenly a loud and strident voice squawked over the
speaker above me: "Whatsa matter? Can't you read? You
gotta pay first!" The tone of voice, more than the words,

embarrassed me, put me on the defensive, made me feel like a fool.

I walked over to the cashier's window and faced a snarling, heavyset woman who was about as cordial as a riled-up pit bull. The look she gave me said, "You are a complete nitwit, and it's a shame I have to put up with people like you." I gave her my credit card, hurried back to my car, filled up with gas, and left—feeling irritated and abused by the encounter.

No doubt I was wrong. I should have read the instructions more carefully and known that I had to pay first. But I goofed—and paid dearly for it! That woman pounced on my mistake with a vengeance that still disturbs me when I think about it.

But her response typifies a whole style of relating to other people that is far too common among us. It is a relational style marked by irritation, criticism, and a haughty self-righteousness. If we are honest, we would all have to confess that we have joined company with that woman on many occasions. To our husband or wife or kids, we have been a snarling pit bull of condemnation.

All that I have written so far (and all I will write in the pages ahead) is an attempt to move us away from such harsh collisions. As we learn some new principles for relating to people—denying self, avoiding temper tantrums, allowing people to be ordinary, and getting out of the "change business"—we can make our collisions more tender and loving.

In this chapter we will consider another such principle. It goes hand in hand with what I have written in the preceding chapters and is another key piece to this puzzle of loving relationships. We will consider here the necessity of forgiveness, the need to forgive those ordinary, change-resistant people we rub shoulders with daily. Without a spirit of forgiveness in our lives, we are destined for some rough and abrasive collisions.

## Beyond Scorekeeping

In his book *Six Hours One Friday* Max Lucado tells of a letter once sent to our government. The handwriting was shaky. The stationery was lined, loose-leaf paper. The note was dated February 6, 1974. It read: "I am sending $10 for blankets I stole while in World War 2. My mind could not rest. Sorry I'm late." It was signed "an ex-GI," and there was this postscript: "I want to be ready to meet God."

Evidently this ex-GI is not alone in his guilt. His is just one of thousands of letters the government has received through the years. In 1811 the government established a "Conscience Fund" to handle donations like the one made by the soldier. Each year tens of thousands of dollars are deposited in the fund. The biggest year to date was 1950, when 350,000 dollars were collected.

Some of the gifts are small (one lady mailed in a dollar bill for four pens she had taken from the IRS office where she worked) and some are large. But all are an attempt to have a clean conscience. People like the ex-GI and the IRS worker have learned the hard way that it is no fun to live with guilt and regret.

I have often thought that the church could greatly enhance its effectiveness if somebody would invent a "guilt detector." This would be something like the metal detectors used at airports to detect weapons. We could put the guilt detector at the entrance of the church and, if anyone entered carrying a load of guilt, the detector would start beeping or squealing (I suspect it would be beeping and squealing constantly!). Then the person couldn't leave the church unless that burden was unloaded, unless that person experienced the wonder of God's rejuvenating grace. Wouldn't it be great if people could have their burdens lifted at church? Wouldn't the church be a more redemptive place if it could identify the specific guilt people carry and then place the soothing ointment of God's love on that guilt?

But there is no such guilt detector, and I don't foresee one anywhere in the immediate future. This means that we just won't know the guilt that people have to carry with them through life. But my experience tells me that many people carry a burden so heavy that it literally destroys their joy. They would like to dance through life, but guilt makes them drag along one weary step at a time. Unlike the apostle Paul, who said he was able to "forget those things which are behind," most people are haunted by the past. And they will never be able to dance until they experience forgiveness—from God and from another human being.

If we settle into a relational stance of "scorekeeping," we will doom both others and ourselves to misery. When we keep score in our relationships, we remember wrongs, hold grudges, harbor anger, and seek retaliation. It is a common way of relating to people, perhaps even the *most* common way in our culture. When wronged, scorekeepers will tally the point and hold it in unforgiveness.

If we are ever going to set people free, and if we are ever going to master the art of tender collisions, we will have to move beyond scorekeeping and learn to forgive. Forgive our loved ones for being ordinary. Forgive our friends even though we would rather change them. Jesus even commands us to forgive our enemies and to pray for those who would take advantage of us. And forgive them not only because they need the healing balm of grace, but also because we can't live with joy if we have an unforgiving attitude. The price of unforgiveness, in terms of our own joy, is just too high to pay.

## The Deadly Dynamite of Unforgiveness

One time on the old "Amos 'n Andy" radio program, Amos was complaining to Andy about the Kingfish always poking him in the chest. Andy had a suggestion guaranteed to solve the problem: "Hide dynamite under your shirt and blow his hand off."

What Andy failed to consider, of course, was the damage that exploding dynamite would do to Amos! True, it might blow off the Kingfish's hand and prevent him from ever socking Amos again. But then again, there might not be any Amos left to sock.

Whenever we choose not to forgive someone, we are "hiding dynamite under our shirt." We assume our unforgiveness will do damage to the other person, and certainly it will. But it will do even more damage to us. When the dynamite of unforgiveness explodes, it does its most deadly work on the one who lights the fuse.

Think for a moment of all the damage that occurs when we refuse to forgive others:

• We close the door to any hope for future reconciliation with a person. Unforgiveness is a steel wall that permanently separates us from the person who offended us. And there will *never* be a reconciliation until we forgive.

• We develop a negative, resentful personality that poisons *all* of our relationships. Not only do we destroy our relationship with the person we refuse to forgive, but we also do damage to our other relationships. To think we can isolate our unforgiveness and have it affect only one relationship is foolish. We're either forgiving or unforgiving, and all of our relationships will be colored by our choice.

• We hurt our physical health, because unforgiveness has definite physical implications. "Scorekeeping" does harm to our blood vessels, heart, and other internal organs. The writer of Proverbs tells us that a merry heart does us good, like a medicine. But the flip side is also true: A bitter, resentful heart leads to physical sickness.

• We do great damage to our spiritual health. An unforgiving attitude even hurts our relationship to God, because the same door of forgiveness that keeps our mercy *in* also keeps God's mercy *out*. When in the Model Prayer Jesus says, "Forgive us our sins as we forgive those who sin against us," he is telling us to throw the door of forgiveness wide open. In doing so we not only forgive those who have wronged us, but we also receive a fresh dose of God's grace for our own sins. A person who forgives shows that he himself has been forgiven. A person who refuses to forgive shows that he has blocked God's grace.

Those four results of unforgiveness ought to show us that the dynamite of resentment is deadly! If we light that fuse, we can expect to reap some devastation from the explosion. But if we learn to forgive, we reap the positive benefits that always come to the merciful. When we forgive, we tear down the wall that divides us from a person, making reconciliation possible. When we forgive, we gradually develop a positive personality that leads to enriching relationships. When we forgive, our blood pressure goes down and our body relaxes. And when we forgive, we open that door of grace that lets God invade our lives as never before.

No wonder Jesus said, "*Blessed* are the merciful."

### Three Facts About Forgiveness

Perhaps all of us would be more merciful if we would just remember three simple facts about forgiveness. If we know these three truths, we will be more motivated to extend grace to the people around us.

*FACT ONE: We have all been wronged.*

Every last one of us has reason to be resentful. Our parents mistreated us when we were young; our husband or wife was vindictive during the divorce proceedings; our children have done unmentionable things that have sullied the family name; our boss gave the promotion to the young woman in the office who is completely incompetent; the people at the church neglected us in our darkest hour; and you can fill in the blanks as to the other specific wrongs perpetrated against you. People have simply not been fair to us, and all too often we have played the role of the scrawny guy at the beach who gets sand kicked in his face by the muscle-bound bully.

*FACT TWO: We all have a simple choice to make.*

In light of fact one, we have to choose our response to those who have wronged us. Reduced to its simplest form, our option is: forgive or resent. We either offer grace to our transgressors or we resort to scorekeeping. There is no other option. We choose to be merciful, or we choose to keep tally sheets and hold grudges.

*FACT THREE: We all have to live with the consequences of that choice.*

Whichever option we take, we are stuck with the results of our decision. If we opt for resentment, then we shouldn't be surprised when the four results of unforgiveness happen to us. We should even expect that we will reap what we have sown. When we sow unforgiveness, we will eventually reap no reconciliation, a negative personality that poisons all of our relationships, a body that is stressed-out and sick, and estrangement from God.

And if we opt for forgiveness—as hard as it is to bestow mercy on people who don't deserve it—we will reap the glorious rewards. We will find reconciliation a distinct possibility. We will develop a kind and gentle spirit that will nourish all of our relationships. We will enable our bodies to relax and be whole. And we will discover that God is a loving Father who longs to give us joy.

Once we know these three facts about forgiveness, we will at least *want* to forgive those who have wronged us. And once we see clearly the truth of fact three, we will be motivated to be more merciful. Given the devastation of unforgiveness and the joy of forgiveness, only a self-destructive fool would ever opt for the former.

## When It's Impossible to Forgive

I don't want to give the impression, though, that forgiveness is easy. I'm making it sound like we can turn forgiveness on and off as simply as we do the light switch in the hallway. And that's just not the case. Forgiving people can be hard. In fact, it can be impossible.

Some of you who are reading this may be growing weary of my pious pontifications about forgiveness. "Easy for him to say," you're thinking, "but he doesn't know the hurt and pain I've been through because of this person. It's real easy to write wonderful words about grace, but real hard to actually forgive someone who has treated you like dirt. I'd even *like* to forgive, but I can't. I can *say* I've forgiven the person, but I know deep in my heart that I haven't. What can I do about this attitude of unforgiveness? I know it's wrong, but I also know I'd be lying to act like everything is okay. What do I do now that I find it impossible to forgive?"

Well, that question is not an easy one to answer, but maybe I can help you find an answer by asking you some questions of my own. If you will honestly ponder these questions, I think you'll know how to deal with your attitude of resentment.

First, do you really *want* to forgive? It's easy to say we want to forgive, but secretly we can get a perverse pleasure out of hating someone. We can clutch resentment so long we would feel emotionally naked without it. So, I ask you again, do you really *want* to forgive the person who has wronged you? Or are you getting some kind of sad satisfaction out of being the offended party?

Second, will you confess your resentment to a trusted friend or counselor? Unconfessed resentment always sours into depression. That is why we need to find someone who will listen to us and take our unforgiveness seriously. If you find it impossible to forgive a person, please find a friend or professional counselor who will listen to your confession and help you unload your bitterness. The worst thing any of us can do with our unforgiveness is to let it fester in silence.

Third, will you pray about your attitude? Pray, if you can, for the person who has hurt you. Pray for your relationship with that person. Pray that God will touch your own heart and soften it. Pray that you will not let one bad relationship spoil your life. If you have the courage to pray seriously about your hurt, I believe God will honor that prayer and bring you healing.

Fourth, are you aware of the damage you're inflicting upon yourself and others by withholding your forgiveness? I believe those four "fruits of unforgiveness" I mentioned earlier will come to any of us who are not merciful. The question is, "Is it worth it?" And the obvious answer is a resounding *no*.

And, fifth, will you look honestly at your own sin? It is not as easy to harbor resentment when you've glimpsed your own sinfulness and faced up to it. If we were without sin, perhaps we could justify our hurt and anger. But since we have inflicted some pain upon others ourselves, shouldn't we temper our attitude with a dose of self-scrutiny? Since none of us is without sin, shouldn't we feel a bit guilty for throwing the stone at someone else?

As I said, there is no quick fix for those relationships where there is deep hurt. No one has a magic potion that can be applied to a wounded soul to make it instantly better. But we can start by asking the five questions I've just listed and then trying to answer them as honestly as we can. If we will look honestly at our resentment, confess it to someone else, pray about it, acknowledge the damage it is doing to us, and face up to our own sin, we are on the way to a forgiving spirit. We may not be all the way home, but at least we've started the journey.

## The Continuous Thread

When you begin reading the New Testament, you are quickly impressed with how much Jesus deals with the issue of forgiveness. It was the continuous thread of his ministry and the recurring theme of his teaching. Wherever he went, Jesus spread the message of forgiveness—God's forgiveness of people and the need for his followers to forgive as well.

• There was the time in Capernaum when Jesus was teaching in a house. Suddenly the thatched roof started to move, and a paralyzed man was lowered into the room where Jesus was. Surely the paralytic and the four friends who had removed the roof were desperate for healing. Surely they would do anything to have his health restored. And how did Jesus respond? He said to the paralyzed man, "Son, your sins are forgiven" (Mark 2:5). A strange thing to say, wouldn't you agree? But Jesus knew that forgiveness, a healing of the spirit, was even more vital than a healing of the body. He went on to cure the man's body, but his first priority was giving the man forgiveness.

• Then one day the religious authorities brought to him a woman who had been caught in the very act of adultery. The law prescribed death by stoning for her sin, and these religious leaders were ready to carry out the law. But when Jesus said, "If any of you is without sin, let him be the first to throw a stone at her" (John 8:7), the men dropped their rocks and left. Then Jesus said to the woman, guilty of awful sin and deserving of harsh condemnation, "Neither do I condemn you. Go now and leave your life of sin" (John 8:11). What she deserved was judgment; what she got was grace.

• That other woman, the one at Simon's house, got forgiveness too. She was also a known sinner, probably a streetwalker, whose presence at a party thrown by a Pharisee was scandalous. But when Jesus heard people murmuring about her sin, he told a story about a forgiving moneylender that underscored the truth he wanted to make: "He who has been forgiven little loves little" (Luke 7:47). Then he turned to the woman and forgave her of all her sins.

• One day Simon Peter, who had been hearing all this talk about forgiveness, asked a very practical question: Just how far does this forgiveness extend? Shall we forgive someone seven times? I'm sure he thought that was a gracious standard, since the rabbis of the day required a person to forgive only three times. But Jesus told Peter to keep on forgiving—"seventy times seven" is the way he put it—and to prop the door of forgiveness wide open all the time.

• Then there were the stories, one after another, about forgiveness. The one about the moneylender who gladly forgave a debt that couldn't be repaid. The one about the prodigal son who blew it but came home to unconditional forgiveness and a party in his honor. The one about the man who was forgiven a debt of millions and then wouldn't forgive his friend a debt of a few bucks. The one about the man who threw a party and invited the last, the lost, and the least. The one about the religious Pharisee and the sinful publican, and how the publican gets justified with God just by muttering a one-sentence prayer for forgiveness. The one about the hard-hearted judge who grants justice to a woman just because of her persistence. Every one of those stories revolves around forgiveness. Jesus was trying, in all of those parables, to tell us the importance of forgiveness, how to receive it from God and then give it away to others.

• Finally, there was his death on the cross. It was ugly, illegal, and cruel. He was forsaken by his friends, forsaken even by God. And what was his concern? What did he say in the midst of his agony? "Father, forgive them..." (Luke 23:34). He died the way he lived, bestowing forgiveness on people. And he did it because he knew that this was what they needed most.

From the beginning of his ministry until his death at Calvary, forgiveness was the passion of Jesus' life. He gave it away to sinners, told stories about it, and died with words of pardon on his lips. And the question for all of us who call ourselves his followers is this: If forgiveness was that important to Jesus, shouldn't it be to us?

## The People of the Late Afternoon

One of the other stories Jesus told was about a landowner who hired some men to work in his vineyard (see Matthew 20:1-16). He hired some workers at six in the morning and agreed to pay them a denarius if they would give him a full day's work. Then the landowner hired some more workers at midmorning, some others at noon, and still others at midafternoon. Finally he rounded up a few more workers just an hour before quitting time.

At the end of the day the workers gathered for their pay. The owner started with the men who had worked just an hour and gave them each a denarius. Those who had worked all day began to wink at each other and smile. If one hour was worth a denarius, what would a whole day be worth? But, much to their surprise and dismay, they too received a denarius.

As you can imagine, they were incensed and began to grumble. "It's not fair. We worked all day in the sweltering heat and got one lousy denarius. These guys saunter in just before quitting time and make the same amount. What gives?"

And the owner replies, "Didn't I tell you I would pay you a denarius for your work? Be happy that I'm fulfilling our agreement. And don't fret about these other men. If I want to be gracious to them, what is it to you? Don't I have the right to do what I want to with my own money?"

Obviously, the men who had worked all day had a legitimate complaint. It really wasn't fair. Those late-arriving workers certainly didn't deserve the same wages as them. But that, I think, is the point Jesus is trying to drive home. His kingdom is not based on the merit system; it is based on *grace*, and grace is never "fair." Grace always pays us far more than we deserve.

But the point I want you to see that relates to our forgiveness of others is this: We either see ourselves as "people of the early morning" or "people of the late afternoon." And which group we put ourselves in determines how forgiving we will be.

If we see ourselves as "people of the early morning," we will be angry that God is not fair. It will anger us that it rains on both the just and the unjust and that we've never been properly rewarded for our virtuous life. We will also be strict "merit system" people and have a hard time forgiving anyone who shows up at quitting time but still gets a full day's pay. "People of the early morning" are righteous, fair, unforgiving—and miserable.

But if we see ourselves as "people of the late afternoon," our whole perspective will be different. If we see ourselves as the guy who showed up at quitting time and got the full day's pay, we will be filled with celebration. We're liable to go running down the road to tell our friends and neighbors, "You're not going to believe this, but I just made a denarius for working one measly hour. Let's go out and celebrate!" "People of the late afternoon" know that God is absurdly generous, and in turn they tend to be generous too. They are grateful, forgiving, and filled with joy.

One of the things that Jesus repeatedly asks us to do in the Gospels is to look honestly at ourselves. We are not to cast the first stone unless we ourselves are sinless. We are not to be angry about the speck in our brother's eye unless we are willing to see the plank in our own eye. We are not to identify with the self-righteous Pharisee, but with the lonely, little publican who knew he was a sinner. Over and over again Jesus calls us to see ourselves as we truly are. And do you know why? Because he wants us to know that we're "people of the late afternoon"! We're all recipients of a divine generosity that we don't deserve. We all receive a lavish paycheck from God, though our work in the vineyard has been insignificant. And we are to live the way "people of the late afternoon" always live—with gratitude, forgiveness, and joy.

### Here in the Real World

Meanwhile, back here in the real world, we are still stuck with ordinary, sinful people. People who have hurt us. People who won't change. People who have made grievous mistakes. People who lug a heavy load of guilt with them everywhere they go. What shall we do with these people? There is only one positive option: Forgive them.

Your ex-husband was abusive to you? Forgive him.

Your kids have done you wrong? Forgive them.

Your preacher ran off with the church organist? Forgive him.

Your daughter had a baby out of wedlock? Forgive her.

Your parents were emotionally cold when you were young? Forgive them.

As difficult as it might be, as bad as the crimes against you might be, you must either resent or forgive. And, as we have seen in this chapter, the cost of resentment, in terms of your own joy, is just too high to pay.

Back here in the real world, you see, the only road to joy always passes through forgiveness.

---

> *We can make our collisions tender if we quit keeping score and instead forgive other people.*

# 7

# A Narrow Love

*God has the power to love everyone, but you and I will be doing well to love a handful of people. We can be friendly with the masses and kind to the multitudes, but we can love only a few people. Real love demands so much time and energy that we'll be hard-pressed to love even a few.*

*The song on the radio* the other day said it well. The singer was hurt and bewildered because the woman in his life had walked out on him, and he didn't know why. He ran through a mental checklist: He hadn't cheated on her; he hadn't lied; he hadn't done anything to justify her leaving. And then the reason for her departure hit him like an 18-wheeler: It's not what he *did*, it's what he *didn't* do. He didn't hold her, didn't tell her he loved her, just assumed she knew. Once he sees his mistake, he sings of it over and over: "It's not what I did, it's what I didn't do."

That song is a reminder that many relationships die from simple neglect. Some relationships are ruined because of some specific, overt action, but many just wither in time because of inattention. Some marriages, for example, are damaged because either the husband or wife has an affair, but far more often a marriage is poisoned by simple neglect. Some go down in one fell swoop, but usually the marriage is killed one neglectful day at a time. The epitaph over many failed marriages could easily read: It's not what they did, it's what they didn't do.

## Narrowing the Focus

I have some bad news for you: You cannot love the whole world. We have been told all our lives that we're supposed to "love everyone," but in truth, none of us can pull it off. God has the power to love everyone, but you and I will be doing well to love a handful of people. We can be friendly with the masses and kind to the multitudes, but we can truly *love* only a few people. Real love demands so much time and energy that we'll be hard-pressed to love even a few.

Once we realize this, though, we can narrow our focus and begin to concentrate on those few. We don't have to feel guilty that we're not loving the world or ministering to the needs of mankind. We can, instead, feel the freedom to start where we are and aim our love at some specific people.

I take heart when I look at the strategy of Jesus in the Gospels. He basically focused his life on 12 men. He conversed with others, healed many sick people, and

taught the multitudes, but his primary ministry was to
12 men. He traveled with them, shared meals with them,
taught them about God, and opened the door of his
deepest self to them.

Why would he adopt such a strategy? Why, in a world
with so many needs, would he limit himself to 12 ordinary people? I think it was because he knew that this was
the only way to reach the whole world! He gave himself
to those 12 men so that you and I and the rest of the world
could eventually be saved. It certainly didn't seem to be
the most spectacular or expeditious strategy he could
have employed, but ultimately it was the most effective.

Jesus' strategy was shocking in its simplicity. As far as
we know, he never submitted an impressive budget to
his followers. He never held any political office or was
granted any pompous titles. He never wrote a book,
built a building, or sought the respect of the authorities.
He never passed any revolutionary legislation or assembled an army of crusaders. What he did was so simple
that it changed the world: He loved a few people boldly.

His strategy even to this day seems unimpressive to
us. We're still attracted to people with titles, degrees,
and salaries that run to six figures. But to every generation the gospel retells the story of Jesus and his "naive"
plan of narrowly focused love. And the most telling sign
that his plan worked is that now, 2000 years after he put
his plan into effect, we are still talking about him, still
mystified by his strangely wonderful life, and still convinced that he was the Son of God and the Savior of the
world.

And what did he leave behind when he died on the
cross? No buildings. No books. No money. No creden-
tials. Just a handful of people whom he had loved in

specific ways. But that legacy was enough! What he did to Peter, James, John, and the others who experienced his love was enough to tilt all of history toward God. You and I today are but the latest of millions who have believed because Jesus chose to devote himself to a small group of people.

## The Truest Test of Faith

Since "narrow love" was the strategy Jesus used while he was on earth, we shouldn't be surprised at all at his statement in Matthew's gospel about the Great Commandment (see Matthew 22:37-40). A religious leader asked him to pinpoint the greatest commandment in all the law. It was a trick question, for who would be able to pick just one out of all the laws in the Old Testament?

But Jesus was up to the task and said the greatest commandment has two parts. First, love God with all you have and are. Second, love other people as you love yourself. In other words, the greatest commandment is about *relationships*. The truest test of our faith is our relationship with God and our relationship with people. Jesus even said that all the law and prophets hang on these two prongs, that the whole Old Testament revolves around these two statements.

Now, with the Great Commandment still ringing in our ears, let me ask you a personal question: How's your spiritual life? The answers we are prone to give to that all-important question typically evade the issue. When we try to evaluate our faith, we often divert our eyes from our relationships and make substitutes for the Great Commandment.

"How's my spiritual life?" we echo. "Great! I don't smoke, drink, cheat on my taxes, or run around on my

spouse. I know I'm right with God because my morality is above reproach."

Well, there's no doubt that we all need to be as moral as we can be. I too don't do any of the four "no-no's" listed above. But I also know that morality is no substitute for the Great Commandment.

"How's my spiritual life? Couldn't be better! I've memorized lots of Scripture, I believe in the virgin birth and deity of Christ, I know the arguments for the existence of God and the historicity of the resurrection, and I've mapped out my own theory for the second coming. It's sad to me that most Christians are so ignorant of important doctrines."

True, doctrine is important to us as Christians. And true, it's impossible to live right if we don't think right. But it's also true that orthodoxy is no substitute for the Great Commandment.

"How's my spiritual life? Super! I've been going to church every week, even on Sunday night. I'm teaching a Sunday school class and serving on the finance committee. My whole life has gotten wrapped up in the church, and I feel so much better because of it."

I too know that the church is crucial to our spiritual growth. Most of us simply will not mature without some involvement with the church. Since I pastor a church, I am at church every time the doors are open, and I frequently encourage other people to get more active in our congregation. But I also know that ecclesiology is no substitute for the Great Commandment.

No, as important as morality, orthodoxy, and ecclesiology are, they are not the truest test of our faith. They can even be good hiding places that keep us from true spiritual growth. As long as we can hide behind our good character, our impeccable doctrine, and our exemplary church attendance, we don't have to face up to the truth about our relationships. We can go merrily on our way, hiding from the two-pronged question that is the truest test of our spiritual condition: *Am I getting closer to God*, and *am I getting closer to a few other people?* The real test of our faith doesn't involve morality, orthodoxy, or ecclesiology; it involves *intimacy*.

## Reasons for Neglect

Since Jesus made "narrow love" the strategy of his life, and since he included loving people as part of the greatest commandment, why don't we do a better job of loving others? Why don't we follow his cue and begin to focus our love on a few people? What keeps us from intimacy? I think there are probably three answers to those questions, three reasons why our relationships are not more loving.

First, we are too selfish. Instead of regularly asking the revolutionary question "What can I do today to make life better for this particular person?" we are prone to ask "What should this person do today to make life better for *me?*" As I mentioned before, we can never really love until we get the spotlight off of self. And we will never begin to concentrate on our husband or wife or children or friends as long as our primary concern is our own welfare. *Self*-centeredness precludes love; *other*-centeredness encourages it.

Second, we get careless. That is, we just forget how important our narrow love is to the people around us. We forget that unless we love them in a concentrated way, they will wither and die. We forget that people with empty "love tanks" inevitably get depressed and desperate. We just get careless and start thinking that television, football games, yardwork, and job promotions are the most important things in life. That is why we need to reread the Great Commandment from time to time, just to keep our priorities straight. The most important duties I have are 1) to love God and grow closer to him and 2) to love that woman I committed myself to 20 years ago, to love that daughter who will soon be off to college, to love that son who is moving from boyhood to manhood, to love those parents who have nurtured me all my life, and so on. The Great Commandment forces me to reexamine my priorities and make sure that I'm not giving my best time and energy to peripheral matters.

Third, we get busy. Narrow love does take time and energy. It cannot be squeezed between work and the ball game on television. If we add up the hours that we have already committed to work, sleep, and extracurricular activities, we will see that we just don't have much time to love people. Once we decide that narrow love is going to be the strategy of our life, we may have to make some radical changes on our personal calendar. Once we commit to really loving a few people, we might have to drop some extracurricular activities. We might even have to change jobs. But whatever changes we have to make will be worth it if they enable us to get our priorities right. What is important to us? Family? Friends? Parents? Then why don't we live like it?

### Declarations of a Narrow Love

When we decide to make narrow love our priority, we will discover that it has several subcomponents. Saying

"I'm going to start focusing my love on this particular person" is just the starting place. That commitment will actually be expressed only when we make some more specific declarations. Here are some promises we will have to make to ourselves if we're going to narrow our love.

**1.** *I will begin to communicate with this person in a deeper way.* That declaration means two things. First, it means I will begin to pay attention to this person's life—what she's saying and doing. I will seek to know her hopes and hurts. I will listen to her when she talks. I will take her life seriously. Second, it means I will share myself with this person. I will tell her my own hopes and hurts. I will tell her what I did today and what I hope to do ten years from now. I will "come out of hiding" and let myself be known to her, and in the process I will give her permission to do the same. It is both sad and amazing that we can live under the same roof with people and not even know who they are. The fact is that we will go to our grave not knowing who they are unless we take the initiative to deepen the communication.

Eugene Peterson in his book *The Contemplative Pastor* says we use three kinds of language when we speak with others. Language I is the language of intimacy and relationship. Language II is the language of information. Language III is the language of motivation. He laments the fact that Language I is becoming more and more obsolete in our culture:

> Languages II and III are clearly the ascendant languages of our culture. Informational language (II) and motivational language (III) dominate our society. We are well-schooled in

language that describes the world in which we live. We are well-trained in language that moves people to buy and join and vote. Meanwhile Language I, the language of intimacy, languishes.

One of the best ways to narrow our love is to notice which kind of language dominates our conversations. Only as we begin to use Language I can we hope to put more love into our relationships.

2. *I will be present for this person's significant events.* That means I'll be there for the ball game or the band concert. I'll be there for the graduation or the wedding. I'll be there when sickness comes or his loved one dies. There is simply no substitute for physical presence in a relationship. Just being there says volumes to a person, and we don't have to say a word to show people we think they're important. We just have to be present when significant events in their life are marked.

Recently I asked a friend what helped her most as she mourned the loss of her father. "Friends just being there—at the funeral, at Mother's house—helped more than anything," she said. That seems awfully simple, doesn't it? Just being there. But that is one of the simple, profound truths we must learn if we want to narrow our love. If you want to grow closer to your husband, just be there for his company party or bowling league. If you want to grow closer to your kids, just be there for the school party or the Vacation Bible School commencement. In fact, if you want to grow closer to anyone, just make it a priority to be there for their important events. When it comes to building good relationships, you cannot overestimate the importance of your presence.

3. *I will give this person the best of my time and money.* I once read how many hundreds of thousands of dollars it costs a parent to get a child from birth through college. The amount was mind-boggling! But how better could we invest our money? And how better can we ever invest our time and money than in the people we love? This third vow will keep us from offering people "leftovers"— the time left over after work, golf, and PTA, and the money left over after the new car and the Caribbean cruise. When I make the promise that a person will get the best of my time and money, I'm saying that my vow of narrow love is more than words. I'm putting my time and money where my mouth is!

Last Valentine's Day we gave our 14-year-old son a Valentine with a note in it. The note read: "This coupon entitles you to one baseball bat." A few days later he redeemed that coupon at the local sporting goods store. That Valentine ended up costing us almost 60 dollars! He got a super-duper Easton aluminum bat that would do a major leaguer proud.

However, that bat is already proving to be a good investment—not just because it is a high-quality bat, and not just because my son can use it with pride in his Pony League, but because it will give us occasion to spend a lot of time together. This very afternoon we're heading to the batting cage so he can take some swings. Tomorrow we will cart it to the Pony League tryouts. Throughout the season we'll use that bat to hit grounders in the backyard, take swings at the batting cage, and experiment with stances that will increase his batting average. In short, that bat will serve as glue that will stick us together.

I suppose a seven-dollar bat from K-Mart could accomplish the same thing. But my point is that any money or time we can invest like that is a fine investment. Narrow love demands that we give our loved ones the best that we have and the best that we are. And, practically speaking, it means that we give them both our time and our money.

4. *I will suffer with this person.* Every relationship is an invitation to suffer. When we bring a tiny baby into this world, we are filled with expectancy and joy. But if we are wise, we also know that this bundle of new life will cause us to suffer. Before that child is grown, we will spend some sleepless nights with her trying to ease her colic, cry with her when she scrapes her knee, agonize with her over the prospect of kindergarten, hold her hand when she goes into the hospital for surgery, mourn with her when she loses the election at school, lament with her the loss of a boyfriend, and so on. Even when she is grown, we will perhaps join her in the labor room to help her give birth to her own child or give her our support when she goes through a divorce.

You see? That little bundle of new life will inflict much suffering upon us! And so will any person we choose to love. Every child, every spouse, every friend is an invitation to suffer, and we can love those people only if we're willing to accept the invitation.

5. *I will take delight in this person.* We do a wonderful thing for people when we give them the gift of our delight. To take delight in people means our eyes light up when we see them coming! When I make this fifth vow, I'm pledging to take delight in my wife, my children, and a few special friends. They will know when they see the look in my eyes that they are valued—not because

they're beautiful, talented, or intelligent, but because they're alive and special to me.

And just how do we communicate this delight to others? In small, ordinary ways. We listen to them, laugh with them, take them to lunch, remember their birthday, call them on the phone just to chat, try to put into practice the simple principles I'm suggesting in this book. In a thousand different ways we say to the significant people in our lives, "I take delight in you."

Those five declarations keep our love from being some kind of nebulous and wistful pipedream. They are a tangible "action plan," and once we begin to live those declarations our strategy will begin to imitate Jesus' strategy. We will be putting narrow love into action.

## Tending to Relationships

In my earlier book, *Regaining Control of Your Life*, I made a suggestion that to my knowledge has never been heeded. I suggested that across America when a baby is born in one of our hospitals we immediately tie a wrist tag on that child. The wrist tag would have this message on it: "For proper development, this person must be touched, kissed, talked to, listened to, prayed for, and given utmost attention. Unless this person is the object of someone's delight, this person will wither and die." I further suggested that the person be required to wear that wrist tag all through life.

That way those of us who tend to forget can remember our first charge. When that child ventures off to kindergarten, we could look at the message on that tag and be reminded that this little child will never make it through the maze of school life without our focused attention.

When this person becomes a pimply-faced, insecure adolescent, we would remember that our concentrated love is the one ingredient needed for him to move successfully through this stage of life.

When this person marches to the altar and commits matrimony, we could look at the tag again and remember that young married people are dizzy with confusion and need the assurance of someone's delight.

When this person passes through the now-famous midlife crisis, we could peek at the tag again and remember that grown people need love as much as infants.

And when this person checks into the nursing home, we would look at the tag and know that our love is as crucial as ever, that without it this person will latch onto the nearest disease and die.

If nothing else, that wrist tag would remind us that relationships are dynamic. They must be tended—daily! If we don't tend our relationships, they will die. If we get too selfish, careless, or busy and don't focus our love on specific people, we will likely survey the wreckage of a relationship that crashed. And we will join the singer in his mournful lament: "It's not what I did, it's what I didn't do."

### A Simple Set of Instructions

The scene is a familiar one: A father works feverishly on Christmas Eve assembling a bicycle for his child. He began the task with enthusiasm and pride, for assembling a bicycle on Christmas Eve is an American ritual and a commonly accepted badge of fatherly love. And he began with confidence, for after all, how hard can it be to bolt on a couple of wheels, slide a handlebar into place, and put a seat on a frame?

The answer, he discovers around midnight, is: *Plenty hard*. What looked like a simple project becomes a nightmare of twisted chains, missing screws, and parts that don't quite fit. What started out as a joyful fatherly deed turns into an exasperating ordeal punctuated by unprintable mutterings of unbelievable frustration. And of course the deadline is drawing near. Some time before the sun peeks over the horizon his little Matthew or Molly is going to come tearing into the living room to see what Santa has delivered. The longer the night grows, the shorter father's temper becomes.

Then he discovers something he hasn't noticed before. There in the box is a folded piece of paper. In desperation he picks it up and casts a weary eye at it. "Instructions for Assembly" it says in bold letters at the top. Because he is ready now, at two o'clock in the morning, to admit his ineptitude, he decides to give these instructions a go. He disassembles the unrecognizable pile of wheels and pedals before him and starts over with step one. Slowly and carefully he proceeds through the instructions, until finally a full-fledged bicycle takes shape before his sleepy eyes. What a joy! Somewhere around 4 A.M. he shuffles off to bed, proud of his achievement and secure in the knowledge that his offspring will be delighted at the wonder Santa hath wrought.

That scene is both sweet and amusing—unless *you* happen to be the father in the picture. If you are the lughead who can't even put a simple bicycle together, it is not a funny thing. I myself can bear testimony that what you feel in that situation is not humor but pure, unvarnished exasperation. Let it hereby be known to all that I have already worn that badge of fatherly love and will never again display my mechanical stupidity by trying to assemble anything for anyone on Christmas Eve.

I show you that picture of parental frustration because it seems to me a parable of what is happening to many of us as we try to build a life of joy. Years ago we were given a life, of all things, and told to assemble it into something pretty and useful. Since most of us are reasonably intelligent and creative, and since most of us have plenty of initiative, we started the project with confidence and pride. After all, how hard can it be to get to know God, or to build loving relationships with people, or to find fascination, or to use money wisely? How hard can it be, really, to build a life of joy?

The answer, some of us are starting to think, is: *Plenty hard*. We learned early to walk and talk and flush. We got a fine education. We established dozens of relationships. We got a job and made a nice pile of money. We got married, perhaps, and had a couple of beautiful children. In short, we did everything we thought necessary to give ourselves "the good life."

But now, much to our surprise and dismay, we're starting to feel like that father at two o'clock in the morning. We're starting to fear that our way of constructing a life may not be the right way, that our best insights and abilities have produced a tangled mess of existence that is neither pretty nor useful. We're getting the nagging suspicion that to build what we want to build, we're going to need a midcourse correction.

When we cast a weary (and wary!) eye around us for some help, we are overwhelmed by the options available to us. Our neighbor is into reincarnation and has a couple of books she wants us to read. Our "freed-up" friend at work says we need an "open marriage" to broaden our sexual horizons. Our brother-in-law, who runs marathons, tells us we need a fitness program. Someone else suggests we're under too much stress and need to try some relaxation techniques. The psychologist who works down the hall says that we've never learned to be our own best friend. The preacher on the radio says we need to start tithing—preferably to his ministry. The expert on the television talk show tells us our biggest problem is our failure to communicate with our children.

It's perplexing, isn't it? When we begin to fish around for help in building a life of joy, we quickly become dizzy from all the good advice people are most willing to bestow upon us.

What I'm suggesting in this chapter is that we throw away that long list of good advice and go back 2000 years to a simple set of instructions Jesus left us. Both in the strategy of his life (narrow love) and his teachings (the Great Commandment), he gave us a simple pattern for building a life of joy. We are to shed nonessentials and spend our lives growing intimate with God and people. That's it. As unimpressive and naive as that sounds, those are the two priorities Jesus gave us.

And since the primary purpose of this book is to make your collisions with other people more tender, I have stressed the second of those priorities in this chapter. We are to quit loving "in general" and start loving "in particular." God has entrusted to each of us six, ten, twelve people who are our "primary assignment" here on earth. Our calling is to shower them with both attention and affection. Spend time with them. Take delight in them. Fill their "love tanks" with the high-octane fuel of our concentrated care.

If we will do that—if we will adopt a personal policy of narrow love—we will not only be following Jesus, but we will also receive two wonderful benefits.

First, we will get the joy of seeing our loved ones "come alive." Narrow love works miracles in the hearts of people.

Second, we will discover that focusing our love does something miraculous in our own heart. There will be a lightness and happiness within us that we haven't felt in a long time.

That father who assembled the bicycle that night? His eventual satisfaction on Christmas morning is nothing compared to the thrill of narrowing our love and then watching the results.

> *We can make our collisions tender if we narrow our focus and love a few people in specific ways.*

# 8

# *The Magic Touch*

*It's hard to fathom that just touching people can bring about healing. It might be even harder to envision ourselves as "huggy, touchy" people when we've carefully cultivated an image of reserved respectability all of our lives. But it is possible that being reserved and distant has led us to relationships that are not full of much love.*

We have a cat at our place. She wandered in eight or nine years ago and shortly thereafter declared herself the reigning matriarch of the household. She pretty much calls the shots, and the rest of us step to her command. She tells us when she wants food, when she wants to go outside, and when she is ready for a drink of water. She will only drink, of course, from the dripping faucet in the back bathtub.

We named her "Critter" when she arrived, but in retrospect we should have given her a more elegant name. "Critter" is definitely beneath her. Had we known then what we know now, we would have named her "Isabelle" or "Miranda"—something more in keeping with her pompous, stately style.

Like most cats, ours is private and aloof. But she has a regular ritual that seems out of character with her stand-offish nature. Several times a week she will see me lying on the bed reading a book and come begging for my attention. She'll crawl up on my chest, nuzzle the book out of the way, and say, "Listen, you've been ignoring me, and I'm tired of it. I need you to scratch behind my ears and rub under my chin." So for ten or fifteen minutes I'll let her lie on me, her face next to mine, while I pet her. Then, her "touch quotient" evidently satisfied, she'll stretch, yawn, and saunter into the other room.

I have wondered at times what motivates her to seek human touch like that. Is there something about touch that soothes her, satisfies her, even heals her? Does she instinctively know that touch is good for her, that without it she will descend into some kind of cat depression? I don't really know. But I do know that "Critter" definitely wants to be touched and that she can be quite obstinate about requesting it.

## The Need to Be Touched

A study once conducted at UCLA concluded that the normal person needs eight to ten "meaningful touches" every day to remain emotionally healthy. The importance of touch to my cat might be a mystery, but the importance of touch to my family and friends has been positively substantiated time after time.

Family counselor Virginia Satir has come up with another formula that underscores the necessity of touch in our relationships. She says that it requires four hugs a day for a person to survive, eight hugs a day for a person to maintain emotional health, and twelve hugs a day for a person to thrive and grow. If her formula is anywhere near the truth, most of us need to do a lot more hugging, don't we?

Leo Buscaglia, in his book *Loving Each Other*, quotes Dr. David Bresler, director of the Pain Control Unit at UCLA:

> We can all benefit by learning to express and meet our physical needs in a loving, caressing way. Thus, I give many of my patients a homework assignment: During the upcoming weeks, they are to get and give four hugs a day. I even write out a formal prescription that says simply, "Four hugs a day—without fail." Don't ever underestimate how powerful this therapy can be, and the role it can play in the healing process. And it's a safe prescription too. To my knowledge, no one has ever died of an overdose of hugging. However, as one of my patients told me, "It is addicting. Once you start hugging, it's a hard habit to break!"

Seems like a silly prescription, doesn't it? It's hard to fathom that just touching people can bring about healing. It might be even harder to envision ourselves as "huggy, touchy" people when we've carefully cultivated an image of reserved respectability all our lives. But it is possible, you know, that being reserved and distant has led us to a bunch of relationships that are not full of much love.

The studies say that the people around us need to be touched in loving, tender ways. And our own experience tells us that our safe, antiseptic approach to people has given us a disappointing assortment of safe, antiseptic relationships. So, if people need to be touched, and if we need to touch people to grow closer to them, why don't we begin to find some natural ways to touch those we love?

## The Most Personal Sense

We run from touch because is it the most intimate of all of the five senses we have. If we are afraid of intimacy, we will certainly be afraid of touching people.

Imagine that you have a husband or son who has been a hostage in a foreign country for several years. You have prayed daily for his safe return, wept bitterly over the injustice of his imprisonment, and dreamed of the day he would return home. And then the message finally comes. An agreement has been worked out freeing the hostages in this particular country. Your loved one will be home in a week!

On the day his plane is to arrive, you get to the airport two hours early. Your heart is pounding. You pace the floor waiting for the announcement of the plane's landing. You watch the runway for approaching planes. At long last his plane touches down. A stream of people files off the plane, and then you see him. He looks haggard and thin. But he's alive and well and walking toward you with a silly grin on his face.

At that point you have five senses available to you to

express your love to him. All five are needed to communicate what you feel at that moment, but only one is personal and intimate enough to truly capture your feelings.

You have your sense of smell, and you will use it to inhale his fragrance—the pungency of his aftershave, the sweetness of the mint in his mouth, the smell of his leather jacket. But you will do more than just sniff your loved one. Your sense of smell cannot communicate your feelings at that wonderful moment of reunion.

You have your sense of hearing, too, and it will serve you well in your celebration. You will listen to his voice, the voice you've been dreaming of hearing for so long. You will hear his words of welcome and your own words of unrestrained glee, and what you hear will bring you great joy. But your sense of hearing is not going to be the primary sense you rely on in your time of ecstasy.

You have your sense of taste, and it will help you as you kiss him and then drink coffee and down a doughnut in the airport lobby. But taste is not the sense that most communicates what you want to communicate to your loved one.

You have your sense of sight, and it will be one of the best senses available to you in that situation. You will use it to watch for arriving planes, to scan the people filing into the lobby, to pick out your husband or son as he searches eagerly for you. You will use it, too, to assess his condition. Somewhat pale. Slightly underweight now because of his ordeal. But still him. Still that same silly smile. Still parts his hair the same way. Still walks like a penguin. Your sense of sight will be a joy to you there at the airport, but it is not the best sense you have available to you, either. Can you imagine how frustrating it would be to just gawk at your loved one from a distance, to stand aloof and coldly assess what your eyes tell you about him?

No, though those four senses would all play a part in the reunion, only the fifth sense would adequately communicate what needs to be communicated. You would have to use your sense of touch, because touch is the most intimate and personal of the senses. You would run to him, throw your arms around him, kiss him, rub your hands through his hair, slap him on the back, hold his hand, and in a dozen other ways touch him. Without touch, you just could not celebrate properly. You simply could not communicate your love to your husband or son if you could not touch him. Without touch, you would have to be resigned to smelling, tasting, hearing, and seeing him. But those four senses together cannot communicate love as eloquently as the sense of touch.

We instinctively know that touch is the most personal of the senses, and we reveal that knowledge all the time. When we are angry with a person, for instance, we don't mind looking at that person or listening to that person. But we don't want to touch that person. Touch says something we don't want to say when we're mad— unless the touch is harsh and violent! Tender touch— holding a hand, giving a back rub, hugging—is the deepest way we humans can express our love to another. And when we are angry at someone, we just can't be hypocritical enough to touch him.

And, of course, the most personal and sacred of all relationships—the sexual relationship between a man and a woman—is primarily a relationship of touch. When God fashioned men and women and gave them the capacity to build a permanent bond of sexual love, he made touch the primary sense for expressing that love.

But still we are prone to forget how important touch is to our relationships. Books on communication tell us how to talk and listen; seldom do they tell us how to touch. We learn how to "share our deepest self" and how to do "active listening." But until we learn how to naturally and softly touch people, our relationships will stay cold and distant. Without the magic of tender touch, our collisions will remain abrasive.

## A Velvet Hand in an Iron Glove

Desmond Morris in his book *Intimate Behavior* writes:

> Unhappily, and almost without noticing it, we have gradually become less and less touchful, more and more distant, and physical untouchability has been accompanied by emotional remoteness. It is as if the modern urbanite has put on a suit of emotional armor and, with a velvet hand inside an iron glove, is beginning to feel trapped and alienated from the feelings of even his nearest companions.

I am haunted by that phrase "a velvet hand inside an iron glove." That phrase seems to capture the way many of us relate to people these days. We still have a velvet hand of love and intimacy, but we cover it with an iron glove of distance and detachment that renders our relationships cold. Why don't we just take that iron glove off and begin to bless people with a velvet touch?

Years ago I read about the Zulu tribe in South Africa. This "primitive" tribe has some fascinating customs. When a child is born, that child is breast-fed by its mother and then carried on the mother's back, skin to skin, for two years. The Zulu child is given more physical contact in two years than most American children will receive in ten.

Then that child is placed on the ground but continues to get a lot of touching. Not only mother and father, but older children in the culture carry the younger ones and give them affection. Other Zulu adults, "mamoos" and "dadoos," also care for the child, so that the little Zulu is constantly being held and touched.

But of course those primitive Zulus seem awfully "backward" to those of us in modern America. We have our own system for raising children, and it is a far cry from the Zulu system.

In our culture when a baby is born, that baby is given a sterile bottle and then scuttled off to a babysitter or day care center while mom and dad work. Even if that baby is kept at home, mom has so much to do that she can hardly find time to hold him, let alone cart him around on her back for two years. That baby will be held some and cuddled some, but the chances are good that he will receive about as many negative touches as positive ones.

Then that child ventures off to kindergarten, where he becomes one of 20 kids vying for the teacher's attention. If he gets touched at all, it will likely be a blow to the stomach from the class bully at recess. And so it goes throughout his childhood. He is loved, but seldom touched. He plays ball, makes decent grades, attends church, and is generally "a good kid." But no one focuses on him, touches him, teaches him how to fish or play chess. He grows up loved at a distance.

Eventually he becomes an adolescent and spends hours staring at a television or playing video games. About the only real physical contact he has are the pokes on the arm or the shoves he gets at school. No one who really loves him has the time or interest to give him a "high five" or wrestle with him on the living room floor or wake him up with a back massage. He moves into adulthood with his "touch tank" on empty.

Probably he will fall in love with a girl and ask her to marry him. During the courtship, he will touch and get touched as never before. But after the marriage he will revert to what he knows best—love at a distance. He will gradually quit touching his wife—except for a sexual encounter once in awhile—and she will quit touching him. They will, though, have a baby, and that child will be the pride of their lives. But, creatures of habit that we all are, he and his wife will do all they know to do. They will raise that baby the way they were raised. The bottle. The daycare center. The busy schedule. The velvet hand in an iron glove.

And on and on it will go—one lonely, untouched generation breeding another one just like it. This cycle will never be broken unless individual people change the way they relate to their families. On and on the cycle of detached love will go—until individual people decide to take off the iron glove and throw it away.

I ask you: Which culture would you suppose has the highest crime rate—the Zulu or the American? Which one would you think has the most teenagers on drugs? Which one has the highest suicide rate? Perhaps we sophisticated Americans need to think twice before labeling the Zulus "backward."

## The Plight of the Untouched

The child who grows up the victim of touchless, aloof love will suffer in two ways.

First, he will struggle to stay physically and emotionally healthy. It is easy to see the emotional implications of not being touched. Since touch is the most personal of all the senses, to deprive a person of touch is to deny that person emotional warmth. We would all assume that those Zulu children who are touched constantly would be more emotionally healthy than their American counterparts who get lost in a culture of busyness.

But what is not so easy to see are the physical ramifications of not being touched. The child who is loved at a distance will also be more likely to get physically ill than those Zulu children. Helen Colton in her book *The Gift of Touch* writes:

> ... when a person is touched, the amount of hemoglobin in the blood increases significantly. Hemoglobin is a part of the blood that carries vital supplies of oxygen to all organs of the body—including the heart and brain. An increase in hemoglobin tones up the whole body, helps prevent disease and speeds recovery from illness.

Jess Lair in *I Ain't Much, Baby, But I'm All I've Got* tells of a nurse who began to realize the importance of touch in her treatment of patients. She told him, "I started touching all my patients constantly. I held their hands, patted their shoulders, hugged them, even kissed a few. Right away there was a change on my floor. My patients were less confused and they needed less medication."

Those who are untouched, though, are destined to struggle both physically and emotionally. They are like plants that never receive the rejuvenation of a spring shower. And their plight is especially frustrating because the cure for their ailment lies in someone else's hands—literally! Just as that parched plant cannot send rain into its dying roots, so these untouched people cannot provide themselves the touch they so urgently need.

Second, that untouched child will have to seek touch in other ways, and some of those ways are destructive. Children who grow up in cold, distant homes are likely to have their "touch quotient" filled in promiscuous sexual encounters. Spouses who struggle in tired, passionless marriages are good candidates for extramarital affairs. And people who have had little tender touch in their past are prone to touch others in violent, criminal ways.

Back in the mid-seventies I served as the chaplain at a children's home in central Texas. This particular children's home served school-age children, and many of its residents were teenagers. Most of the children in this home had been either abused or neglected by their parents, so most of them had never been touched in a loving way.

But did they ever try to make up for it as teenagers! I know adolescents like to touch each other, but the touching among our kids at the children's home was extreme. The boys and girls held hands, hugged, and kissed constantly. When I took them to summer camp each year, I felt like a detective, constantly spying on them to make sure their touching didn't exceed the boundaries of propriety. It was as if they hadn't had their need for touch filled as children, so they were going to make up for lost time as teens. Since they didn't get their eight to ten daily touches early in life, they were overdosing on adolescent petting.

People are so hungry for touch that they will get it one way or the other. They'll either get touched lovingly or they'll get touched violently, illicitly, or destructively. But, one way or the other, they *will* get touched.

The plight of the untouched, then, is a sad one. Heads they lose and get sick, tails they lose and get hurt. But any way they flip the coin, they come up losers.

## Healing the Sick

Do you remember the story? It is recorded in Luke 8:43-48, and it has to do with the power of touch. Jesus was pressing his way through the crowd when a sick woman reached out and touched the edge of his cloak. Immediately, Luke says, the bleeding that had plagued her for 12 years stopped.

But what's interesting is what happened next. Jesus stopped in his tracks and asked, "Who touched me?" The disciples were incredulous. Who could know? they asked. In a crowd so large, with dozens of people jostling to touch Jesus, how could you pick out just one? And, besides that, who cares anyway?

Jesus persisted. "Someone touched me," he said. "I know that power has gone out of me." Then the woman, seeing that she could not go unnoticed, came trembling and fell at his feet. She confessed that she had touched him and that the touch had healed her instantly. Jesus then lauded her faith and told her to go in peace.

"Power has gone out of me." That phrase underscores for us the hidden, healing power of touch. There was something about his touch that healed. Without that touch, the bleeding would have continued. With that touch, she was healed on the spot.

I would not suggest to you that you and I have the same miraculous power of healing that Jesus had. But I would want to suggest that, like Jesus, our touch does have power. We too have the power to heal people. People who are lonely and cold and miserable can be transformed by our touch. The power goes out of us and into that person, and there is a hidden, gradual healing that begins to take place. Without our touch, the pain will continue. With our touch, wholeness can be restored.

What we must do, then, is find a personal and natural way to touch the people in our lives. Touch is not a "technique" for enhancing relationships. If we see it that way, we will give our kids eight hurried hugs and our husband three perfunctory pecks on the cheek and then await the miracle. We will surely be disappointed.

Touch is not a technique, but a testimony. It says, "I value you and want to be close to you." It even says, "I will be vulnerable with you," for touch can always be rebuffed. When we touch someone genuinely, we are making a statement just as eloquent—perhaps even more eloquent—than our flowery words of affection.

So, we touch them—our kids, our husband or wife, our good friends, our parents. We hold their hand, rub their back, massage their neck, grab them in a loving headlock, or touch them in some other natural way that feels comfortable to us. And if no way of touching feels comfortable? Well, we touch them anyway. We make tentative, trembling attempts to reach out and put skin on skin. They will not ask for it, like my cat. They will even be surprised by it, if they are used to us being withdrawn in our love. But they will thrive on it if it is real. And the relationship will get a much-needed injection of tenderness.

## Remembering Minnie

In her book *Mind Song* Donna Swanson has a poem called "Minnie Remembers." The poem achingly captures the plight of the untouched.

> How long has it been since someone touched me? Twenty years I've been a widow. Respected. Smiled at. But never touched... Oh God, I'm so lonely. I remember Hank and the babies. How else can I remember them but together? Hank didn't seem to mind if my body thickened and faded a little. He loved it and he loved to touch it. And the children hugged me, a lot.... Oh God, I'm lonely! God, why didn't we raise the kids to be silly and affectionate as well as dignified and proper? They drive up in their fine cars. They come to my room to pay their respects. They chatter brightly and reminisce. But they don't touch me. They call me Mom, or Mother or Grandma. Never Minnie. My mother called me Minnie. So did my friends. Hank called me Minnie, too. But they're gone. And so is Minnie.

Minnie could be your mother or mine. She could also be your spouse or child or friend. She is representative of all of those people we are supposed to love. We come to those people all dignified and proper, robed in reserved politeness. But what the Minnies in our life need is to be *touched*. They need for us to shed that robe and get real about our love. They need us to stroke, pet, hug, kiss, and caress them back to abundant life. They need to feel the power flow out of us through touch.

Since I started this chapter a few days ago with the story about my cat, she and I have observed our ritual again. This afternoon after my nap, she curled up on my chest and got her customary scratch and rub.

She left me with three thoughts.

First, I am impressed with her knowledge. She *knows* that touch is important to her well-being.

Second, I am amazed at her brazen demeanor. She's not afraid to admit she needs to be touched. Indeed, she demands it.

Third, I am convicted by our time together. I spend ten to fifteen minutes stroking my cat, but feel like I've done a special thing if I give one of my children a two-second embrace. Have I got something backward here?

> *We can make our collisions tender if we learn the importance of touch and make touching a natural part of our relationships.*

# 9

# *Your Laughter Can Heal*

*The idea that laughter can literally heal fascinates us and somehow rings true with our own experience. But we also need to be aware of the curative power of laughter in our relationships. A genuine belly laugh does as much to rejuvenate a relationship as it does to restore physical heath.*

*I*n my book <u>With Love, From Dad</u> I wrote the following letter to my teenage offspring:

Dear Kids,

Did we ever talk about Norman Cousins' book *Anatomy of an Illness*? It seems to me we discussed it at the supper table one evening. But just in case you've forgotten our conversation, let me refresh your memory and remind you in this letter of the necessity of laughter in our lives.

The book details Cousins' recovery from a critical illness. He decided to take his recuperation into his own hands, and tried something medically heretical. He shunned ordinary treatment and opted instead for big doses of vitamins and regular times of laughter. Every day he had a projector brought into his room and watched funny movies. A surprising thing happened: He made remarkable progress! Tests were run "before laughter" and "after laughter," and they always showed a marked improvement following his gleeful sessions at the movies. Cousins is convinced that laughter literally releases a healing potion into our bodies and that it was a prime factor in his recovery.

Now I'm not advocating that you disregard all medical advice and turn to self-healing. Nor do I want you to throw away the aspirin in the medicine chest. But I do want you to remember the power of laughter. I tend to agree with Norman Cousins: I think laughter actually heals. Medical science will no doubt one day verify the old adage in Proverbs: "A cheerful heart is good medicine, but a crushed spirit dries up the bones" (Proverbs 17:22).

One of the things you've done for me through the years is give me reason to laugh. I have found great delight in watching you move from infancy to childhood to adolescence to almost-adulthood. You two have been my main source of merriment, my "funny movies." Even now I can recall some of the things you've said and done and some of the things we've done together, and I have to chuckle. My mind is crammed with hilarious memories. When you leave home, I may have to buy a projector and start watching classic comedies.

It bothers me that the Christian life is so often presented as a drab, somber march. We Christians are so serious! We act like our gospel is bad news instead of the best news unleashed in the world. I think it's time for Christians to start living the Good News, to act like forgiven, liberated adventurers. One of the great poets reportedly wrote in his journal, "Wonder of wonders! I have been to church today and am not depressed." I know the feeling, don't you?

I'm currently reading a book called *The 2000-Mile Turtle*. It's a funny, tongue-in-cheek book, and you can't read it without a grin. One line in the book bears remembering and repeating: "Next to love, laughter is the best answer to the universe."

That's true. If you have love and laughter in your lives, you'll do fine. Whatever destiny hurls at you, you'll be able to survive and even triumph. Circumstances will never defeat you because you have found a potent one-two punch.

As I sit here at the kitchen table and think about my hopes for you, I offer you a simple two-step approach to life: Keep loving, and keep laughing!

Selah!
Dad

## Good Medicine for Relationships

Norman Cousins' book received a lot of attention because its premise was so intriguing. The idea that laughter literally can heal fascinates us and somehow rings true with our own experience. But we also need to be aware of the curative power of laughter in our relationships. A genuine belly laugh does as much to rejuvenate a relationship as it does to restore physical health.

Laughter actually enhances our relationships in five specific ways.

**1.** *Laughter makes us physically and emotionally healthier, so that we can bring more to a relationship.* When I perform a marriage ceremony for a starry-eyed bride and groom, I always remind them that the finest gift they can give each other is the gift of their best self. It is the gift they offer each other at the altar that day, and it will continue to be the gift they offer each other as the marriage unfolds.

That is true for all of our relationships. We are to offer all the people in our lives the gift of our best self, and laughter plays a vital role in getting that self into tip-top shape.

For one thing, it takes the edge off our anger, depression, and other negative emotions. Laughter is that delightful gust of breeze that blows the negative emotions into the background of our personality.

For another thing, laughter does make us more physically fit, so that the physical self we give others is more presentable. Several years ago Dr. William Fry of Stanford University released some information that verified Norman Cousins' experience. He said that laughter aids digestion, invigorates the heart, strengthens muscles, activates the brain's creative capacity, and enhances alertness. All of this with one hearty chuckle!

Because laughter enhances us both emotionally and physically, it equips us to do a better job of loving people. It helps us bring a healthy body and spirit to our relationships.

**2. *Laugher puts "self" in its proper perspective.*** In his book *When I Relax, I Feel Guilty* Tim Hansel tells about the time that things were going poorly for a certain British shipping line. One of Sir John's colleagues was in his office filling the air with gloom and predicting disaster. Sir John said to him, "You've forgotten Rule Number Four."

His colleague responded with surprise, "What's Rule Number Four?"

"Rule Number Four," said Sir John, "is 'Don't take yourself too seriously.'"

"What are the other rules?"

"There aren't any others," Sir John replied.

Self, as we saw earlier, always wants the spotlight, always wants to fret and stew over its predicaments, always wants to be serious about its plight. But laughter puts it in its rightful place. Laughter disputes its claims as center of the universe. It says, "You are not as important as you think, and life is not as serious as you want to believe. Lighten up, and live a little."

If you have ever tried to relate to a gloom-and-doom person who never laughs, you know what a burden that kind of person can be. He is a burden because he hasn't gotten rid of self, and worry about self drags him—and everyone around him—down. Then there are those life-renewing people who *have* gotten rid of self and know how to laugh. They sort of dance through life because they don't have to carry a heavy self everywhere they go. And they have the remarkable ability to help others feel lighter on their feet, too.

Because laughter is a denial of our selfish self, it enhances our relationships and enables us to do a better job of loving others.

3. *Laughter puts "the light touch" on conflict.* Any time there is the possibility of an abrasive collision with another person, laughter helps us soften the potential conflict.

Before this week is out, chances are good that all of us will be given the opportunity to deflect anger by using humor. Perhaps our husband or wife will suggest that we have neglected some necessary family duty. We then have a choice: Get huffy or laugh. We can either get defensive, or we can take the sting out of the remark with humor. Laughter is a sponge that absorbs critical remarks and prevents them from staining a relationship. How can anyone do battle with a sponge? How can the cycle of anger get going if someone stifles it with a chuckle? And how can resentment ever get a foothold if one person in the relationship wants to laugh instead of argue?

4. *Laughter is an eloquent statement of affection.* There are two sure indicators of intimacy in our relationships. The first one is touch. As I discussed in the last chapter, touch is the most personal and intimate of all of our five senses. The people we love most we will touch most. As we saw, one way to deepen our level of intimacy with another person is to begin to touch that person in natural ways.

The second indicator is laughter. The people we love most will also be the people we laugh with most. Laughter is a strong declaration of affection. Think about the times in your life when you have gotten "tickled." Were those times of laughter with friends or strangers? No doubt they were with friends or family, with people you felt especially close to and comfortable with. We typically reserve our laughter, like our touch, for those we love most. For laughter, like touch, is an expression of deep affection.

5. *Laughter expresses faith in the goodness of God.* How do we show we have been touched by the absurd goodness of God? How do we communicate to an unbelieving world the incredible Good News of grace? What do we do to show that grace has penetrated into the inner recesses of our heart? Preach sermons? Certainly. Sing songs? No doubt. Pass out gospel tracts? Perhaps. But probably most eloquently and convincingly, we laugh. Laughter is a deep expression of faith in God. It says, "In spite of crime, war, and worldwide mean-spiritedness, I believe in the goodness and ultimate triumph of God." I would even go so far as to say that until we develop a personal theology of laughter, our witness to the world will be ineffective. How can somber, sad witnesses hope to convince anyone of Good News? And why would anyone want to become a part of a kingdom whose citizens are messengers of gloom and doom?

## A Theology of Laughter

Someone once said that a Puritan was a person who feared that someone somewhere might be having fun. I'm not sure that is an accurate perception of the Puritans, but it is a fairly accurate perception of many modern Christians. Those of us who have committed our lives to Jesus Christ are seen, by and large, as religious party-poopers. Our Christian commitment is associated with severity and frowns, never celebration and laughter.

Perhaps that renowned theologian, Erma Bombeck, can put the matter in proper perspective for us. This piece appeared in her "Wit's End" newspaper column.

In church the other Sunday I was intent on a small child who was turning around smiling at everyone. He wasn't gurgling, spitting, humming, kicking, tearing the hymnals, or rummaging through his mother's handbag. He was just smiling. Finally his mother jerked him about and in a stage whisper that could be heard in a little theater off Broadway said, "Stop that grinning! You're in church!" With that she gave him a belt, and as the tears rolled down his cheeks added "That's better," and returned to her prayers.

We sing "Make a joyful noise unto the Lord" while our faces reflect the sadness of one who has just buried a rich aunt who left everything to her pregnant hamster. We chant "If I have not charity, I am become a sounding brass or a tinkling cymbal." Translated in the parking lot it comes out "And the same to you, fella!"

Suddenly I was angry. It occurred to me the entire world is in tears, and if you're not, then you'd better get with it. I wanted to grab this child with the tear-stained face close to me and tell him about my God. The happy God. The smiling God. The God who had to have a sense of humor to have created the likes of us. I wanted to tell him He is an understanding God. One who understands little children who pick their noses in church because they are bored. He understands the man in the parking lot who reads the comics while his wife is attending church. He even understands my shallow prayers that implore, "If you can't make me thin, then make my friends look fat." I wanted to tell him I've taken a few lumps in my time for daring to smile at religion. By tradition, one wears faith with the solemnity of a mourner, the gravity of a mask of tragedy, and the dedication of a Rotary badge.

What a fool, I thought. Here was a woman sitting next to the only light left in our civilization—the only hope, our only miracle—our only promise of infinity. If he couldn't smile in church, where was there left to go?

As usual, Erma hits the nail squarely on the head. So many of us _do_ wear our faith with the solemnity of a mourner. The world, just looking at our faces, would think we are peddling funeral plots. But her final question disturbs me most. If that little boy can't smile in church, where is there left to go? If the church is not a place to celebrate and if Christians can't make merry, we have lost the heart of our message. If people who know Jesus Christ, who know they have eternal life, and who know that God will eventually triumph can't laugh, who can?

## Come to the Party

One of the books that first opened my eyes to the connection between Jesus and joy was Karl Olsson's book _Come to the Party_. The book is really Olsson's testimony of how he moved from rigorous righteousness to a more joyful commitment. He came to see the Christian life as a grand party, a party that begins the moment we open our heart to Jesus and continues on into eternity. The book is an invitation for all weary, worn-out Christians to come to the party.

Olsson said that, as he shared the gospel of the party with people around the country, he discovered that they fell into four categories.

First, there were those who doubted there was a party. Into this group we could put the atheists, agnostics, and skeptics, as well as those Christians who believe that a life of faith is also a life of drudgery. For those in this first group, talk of a party is nonsense, the wishful thinking of naive people. I suppose we could even say that most of the world falls into this category. They either haven't heard about the party or they've heard but don't believe it's really going on.

Second, Olsson found those who believe that there is a party somewhere, but they're not invited. Into this group we could put those who feel disqualified from the party because of their past and those "unblessed" Christians who are insecure in their relationship with God. The people in this second category actually exempt themselves from the party. They think their sin keeps them out or that God, for whatever reason, keeps them out, so they never get caught up in the merriment. They *have* been invited, but because of their past sin or their current concept of God, they lock themselves out of the fun.

Third, there were those who believe there is a party and they're invited, but they don't deserve to stay. This group would have to include all of those Christian legalists who, to use the apostle Paul's phrase, "fall away from grace." They start the Christian pilgrimage with joy, but eventually succumb to the burden of the law, of religious obligation and routine. They believe there is a joyful party going on, but they are certainly not experiencing it in their own tiring struggle up the ladder of Christian piety. Because their deeds never quite measure up to their expectations, they stay just outside the door of the party. They don't see themselves as "good enough" to get in.

Fourth, he found those who are invited and who also go and stay. Those in this fourth group keep clinging to grace and keep experiencing the joy it always brings. They know they don't deserve to be at the party, that their invitation was not based on merit. So they just relax and celebrate the wonderful absurdity of it all: They are accepted and welcomed because of the loving nature of the Host. The people in this fourth group are "the blessed," Olsson says. They are secure in their relationship with God, and the natural result of that security is a contagious joy.

Obviously, those in this fourth group have little trouble laughing. Those in the other three groups are doomed to frowns and pessimism. If there isn't a party going on, why laugh? If there is a party but you're not on the invitation list, why laugh? And if there is a party but you don't deserve to stay, why laugh? But if there really *is* a party and you're invited, why not go and have a good time? Why not laugh? What else do you do at a party?

## Kim's Story

"That all sounds nice and pious," I can hear the cynic sneer. "But here in the real world my life is not so great. I'm sneezing constantly because of my hay fever, my job bores me silly, and my kids irritate me constantly. Who are you to advocate laughing in such miserable circumstances?"

I too know that it is not easy to laugh these days. It might even be foolish to laugh in light of our problems and the headlines in the morning newspaper. But then I remember that, as a follower of Christ, I'm *supposed* to be foolish. I am to be a fool for Christ, and a part of that foolishness means choosing to laugh, to have the humor of real faith in a good God.

And I keep hearing about people like Kim Jackson. Kim is a 31-year-old woman who lives in Houston. She has an offbeat humor and a winsome laugh that lifts the spirits of everyone she meets. Kim also has incurable cancer.

In a column in the *Houston Post*, Paul Harasim told Kim's story in a piece called "Keep Laughing in the Face of Death." In 1986 Kim and her husband, James, lost their three-year-old daughter, Amber, to cancer of the eye. It was during their daughter's illness that the Jacksons decided to laugh instead of cry.

"Amber was reacting to our down moods—we were crying a lot—and it wasn't doing her any good," James said. "When we started trying to be more cheerful, we noticed it kept her spirits up and it kept our spirits up. So by the time Kim got breast cancer, six weeks after Amber died, we knew how to handle it."

Kim sees their positive outlook as a simple choice. "You can either focus on the good or the bad. You have to use energy for either one, and it seems to make more sense to make you and others happy rather than sad. I'm not saying it's always easy to be up. I get down too, but it just doesn't make any sense to stay that way. We have so little time on earth."

So the Jacksons have chosen to laugh a lot. Kim has lost her hair six times because of her cancer treatments. She occasionally buffs her bald head as if it were a shoe to amuse her co-workers, and when asked about her baldness, she tells people she's making another sequel to "Star Trek." If he's around when the question is asked, James will tell people he's "snatched her bald-headed."

Kim's positive attitude has helped her beat the odds "Medically, we can't account for her being alive," says Cheryl Pope from the cancer center where Kim is being treated. "The only reason she's still alive, we feel, is because she's so optimistic and upbeat."

It only seems natural that Kim has become president of Smiles Against Cancer, a support group for cancer patients. The goal of the group is to provide good times and laughter for those going through the dark night of cancer treatment.

When we read about someone like Kim Jackson, we are filled with admiration. What an attitude! What a contagious spirit! But then the inevitable question must be faced: If someone like Kim can choose to laugh and to enrich other's lives with her joy, why can't we?

### Taking the Pain Out of the Hard Moments

In his book *The Earth Is Enough* Harry Middleton recounts his adventures living with two old men on a hardscrabble farm in the Ozarks. Born and raised in a rigid, military home, Middleton moved as a teenager to the farm and took up residence with Albert and Emerson. There he learned to fish for trout, to tell stories, to love the land, and to appreciate these two old gentlemen who welcomed him into their lives.

And it was there, in relationship to Albert and Emerson, that he learned to laugh. He remembers: "How I loved the sound of their laughter, how good it was to laugh and laugh until you hurt, how the laughter took some of the pain out of the hard moments, the ones that hacked away at you day in and day out, impervious to resolution, to any remedy except that rising sound of the three of us laughing, laughing until we cried."

That, I think, is what Kim Jackson's laughter is all about. Her laughter is taking some of the pain out of the hard moments, both for her and James and their friends as well. Laughter has the remarkable power to do that, to soothe the rough edges of pain and make it bearable.

And for those of us trying to smooth the rough edges off of some relationships, laughter has the power to make our collisions much more tender. When we laugh with people, all of those serendipities of laughter swing into motion. We get healthier and can bring more to a relationship. We put self in its proper place and make a statement about ego. We fend off conflict by deflecting the anger people toss at us. We make a declaration of affection to those we love. And we express our faith in the goodness and grace of God. Laughter, you see, not only has the power to heal the body and to take the pain out of the hard moments, but it also has the power to rejuvenate relationships.

The old adage has it: He who laughs lasts. It is also true to say: He who laughs will have relationships that last. For, as entertainer Victor Borge once said, "Laughter is the closest distance between two people."

---

*We can make our collisions tender if we loosen up and laugh with people.*

# 10

# *Learning from the Father*

*If our system has been inadequate, the question we must ask is: Where can I find a system that works? If our relationships are not what they should be, we must begin to fish around for some help. We must find a relational equivalent to the San Francisco 49ers—a model we can use to build a successful system.*

The San Francisco 49ers came to town a few weeks ago to play our Houston Oilers, and at that time they were the reigning Super Bowl champions.

Prior to the game with the Oilers, the Houston newspapers ran several stories about the 49ers and their success. They interviewed two former Oilers who now play for the 49ers and asked them their opinion on why San Francisco is so successful. Both players responded by praising the 49ers "system." They said the system was the reason the team wins so consistently.

By "system," those players were referring to the way the 49ers organization does things. The system includes the offensive and defensive strategy, the way practices are run, the relationship between coaches and players, the salary structure of the team, the kind of equipment and facilities the team uses, the method of scouting other teams, the method of drafting new players, and other factors too numerous too enumerate. The team's system really encompasses everything the team does. As the standings clearly show, some systems lead to success, and some lead to failure.

If you were suddenly given the opportunity to run a pro football team, you would do well to imitate the system of the San Francisco 49ers. Whatever that organization is doing, it is leading to success.

## A Relationship System

I tell you about the 49ers not to try to get you to be one of their fans, but to drive home a point I want you to see: *A system is crucial to success or failure in any area of life.* Every organization—indeed, every individual person—employs some kind of system, and that system leads to either success or failure.

Take a business, for instance. Some businesses have a system that leads to job satisfaction for employees, product satisfaction for customers, and a nice profit margin in the company's financial ledger. Other businesses have a system that yields grumpy employees, dissatisfied customers, and a ledger written in red ink.

Or consider a family. Some families have found a

system that leads to respect, harmony, fun, and a wholesome atmosphere. The people who come out of this family system are happy and secure. They also know how to establish a healthy family system themselves, so they can pass it along to future generations. Then there are other families that have unknowingly established a system that is destructive. The people in these families are uptight and miserable, and the atmosphere around the house is definitely depressing.

What makes the difference between a successful business and one that fails? Or a happy family and one that is strife-torn? In each case it is the system that is used. For the business, the system includes the pay scale for employees, the hours that must be worked, the way communication is handled around the office, the courtesy shown to the custodians, and even the color of the wallpaper in the office or the kind of typewriter bought for the secretary. For the family, the system includes how meals are served, how holidays and birthdays are celebrated, how money is handled, and even how the den is decorated and how the yard is kept.

What I want you to see is that *we all have a system for relating to people.* Each one of us has devised a system that leads either to relational success or to relational failure. We have learned our system in a variety of ways. Primarily, we have just picked it up from those unofficial teachers I mentioned earlier. We watched our parents, grandparents, brothers and sisters, and friends, and gradually (even unconsciously) we developed a system for our relationships. We have also read some self-help books, learned some psychological theories, watched some television programs, heard some sermons, and profited from past personal experience. In other words, our current system is an eclectic hodgepodge of ideas that we have been assembling all our lives. And it is either a good system that has led us to an abundance of loving relationships or it is a bad system that has led us to more abrasive collisions than we care to recall.

If our system has been inadequate, the question we must ask is: Where can I find a system that works? If our relationships are not what they should be, we must begin to fish around for some help. We must find a relational equivalent to the San Francisco 49ers—a model we can use to build a successful system.

## A Model for Our Relationships

The best place to find that model, in my opinion, is in an old story many of us have heard all our lives—Jesus' story of the prodigal son recorded in Luke 15. That old story commends itself as a model for our relationships for four good reasons.

First, it is a biblical story. That in itself gives it more authority than most models we could try. The story of the prodigal comes from the lips of Jesus, was faithfully transcribed by Luke, and has been a source of instruction and inspiration for 2000 years. At least for those of us who are Christians, this old story has more weight than any of the new theories and models we might want to try.

Second, it is a story about a relationship. The parable of the prodigal son is a story of a father and his two sons. It deals with the very issue we are dealing with in this book: how to relate to someone and how to build a bridge of intimacy instead of a barrier of estrangement. Because it is about a father-son relationship, we can take the relational dynamics in the story and use them as a model for any relationship we need to improve.

Third, it reveals a system that worked. At the beginning of the story the father and the prodigal son are at odds, separated by different philosophies and different goals. But at the end of the story the father and the prodigal are making merry together at a party! Their differences have been resolved, and a joyful reconciliation has taken place. What started out as an abrasive collision has been transformed into a tender reunion. Whatever the father did worked, and therefore can serve as the model we need for our own relationships.

Fourth, it is a story about God's way of relating to people. This, above all, makes the story the model we need. The father in the story is God, so the story reveals how God does relationships. In the story, Jesus is showing us who God is and how God relates to people. What better model could we find than God himself? If Jesus' parable is about how God relates, isn't it the ideal story for us if we want to learn how to relate? When we study the parable of the prodigal son, we are actually studying the way God treats people, and thus we see the divine model for relationships.

### Listening Again to an Old Story

Before I show you the relational dynamics at work in the parable of the prodigal son, let me first refresh your memory and recap the story for you.

Jesus tells us that a certain man had two sons. The younger one, ready to declare his independence and stake his claim in the world, demands that this father give him his share of the estate. The father, surprisingly, complies and divides his property equally between his two sons.

The younger boy heads off with glee for a far country. At long last he is free! And does he take advantage of it! He buys everything his heart desires and lives the life of a king. But, as luck would have it, a famine hits the land and the boy discovers, much to his surprise, that he is out of money and out of luck. That inheritance that was going to last a lifetime didn't last long at all.

In desperation the boy gets a job feeding pigs. He goes from high-roller to hog-slopper in a hurry! But the job doesn't make him enough money even to buy food, and at times he finds himself yearning to eat the scraps he tosses to the pigs.

It doesn't take him long to realize that he is going nowhere fast. The prospect of feeding pigs and going hungry the rest of his life doesn't hold much fascination for him, and he realizes that even the hired servants at his father's house have it better than he does. So he drafts a letter to his father and decides to hand-deliver it and eat some humble pie. The letter reads: "Father, I have sinned against heaven and against you. I am no longer worthy to be called your son; make me like one of your hired men" (Luke 15:18,19). Note in pocket and pride severely hurt, he trudges back down the road that leads home.

The father, meanwhile, has been checking that road every day since his son left. On the day he catches a glimpse of that familiar silhouette dragging itself home, he takes off like a sprinter down the dusty path. He runs toward his wayward son, throws his arms around him, and kisses him.

The son dutifully takes the letter from his pocket and reads it to his father. But the father scarcely pays him any mind. He is so filled with joy that he turns to his servants and says, "Quick! Bring the best robe and put it on him.

Put a ring on his finger and sandals on his feet. Bring the fattened calf and kill it. Let's have a feast and celebrate. For this son of mine was dead and is alive again; he was lost and is found" (Luke 15:22-24). And with that the father and the son begin the celebration.

But there is another son in the story too, and he is not too pleased with what he sees. As he nears the house, he catches the faint strains of music and laughter. He asks one of the servants what is going on, and the servant tells him of his brother's return. When he learns that the party is in honor of the wayward rabble-rouser, the older brother becomes incensed. He storms into his father's presence and breathes fire: "Look! All these years I've been slaving for you and never disobeyed your orders. Yet you never gave me even a young goat so I could celebrate with my friends. But when this son of yours who has squandered your property with prostitutes comes home, you kill the fattened calf for him!" (Luke 15:29,30).

The father can only tell him the obvious: "My son, you are always with me, and everything I have is yours. But we had to celebrate and be glad, because this brother of yours was dead and is alive again; he was lost and is found" (Luke 15:31,32).

There the story ends. But our understanding of what that story has to do with our relationships only begins.

## Factoring the Father's Love

When we look at that story from the angle of improving our relationships, several key concepts surface. The father did at least eight crucial things in the story that made the eventual glad reunion possible. When we factor the father's love, these eight ideas are revealed.

1. *The father never asserted self and never got caught in a power struggle.* Several times, as the story unfolds, the father "denies self" and shuns an ego-centered response. When the young son demands his inheritance, for example, it would have been natural for the father to have bristled at the very suggestion of such a thing. A big, live "self" would have launched into a tirade and defended its rights. The father, however, divided the property and handed over the money.

Then, when the boy returned home, it would have been so natural for the father to have been hurt, angry, vengeful. The selfish response would have been, "You've hurt *me,* and now I'll hurt *you.* You're going to have to pay for what you've done." But the father, amazingly, denied self, welcomed the boy home with open arms, and threw a party in his honor.

When the older brother came in all huffy and bothered by the party in the prodigal's behalf, the father again could have bristled. A selfish self would have chided the older brother for his insensitivity and scolded him for his pettiness. But the father denied that impulse and reaffirmed his love for the older boy as well.

Through the story, the father consistently does the unnatural thing and denies self. He puts his love for his sons ahead of his own ego.

2. *The father never lost his temper and never lashed out at either of his sons.* Goodness knows they deserved it! Both boys were guilty of obvious wrongs. The younger son was guilty of impudence and stupidity, and the older son was guilty of pride and pettiness. On all three of the occasions I have just mentioned the father could justifiably have exploded. When the prodigal demanded his inheritance, the father could have lambasted him for his

immaturity. When he came home, letter of apology in hand, the father could have rejected his repentance and laid the guilt on him. And when the older brother acted so childish at the party, the father could have burned him with angry words of rebuke. But on all three occasions the father held his tongue. When he had to choose between words of contempt and words of conciliation, he always chose the latter.

3. *The father accepted the prodigal even after the boy's character and reputation were tarnished.* The father's acceptance of his son is, in fact, nothing short of unbelievable. Put yourself in that father's place for a moment, and you will see just how incredible that acceptance was.

Your son has taken your money, run away to a distant land, wasted the money on sinful pursuits, sullied the family's name, and generally made a mess of his life and your sanity. Then he comes home and asks that you take him back. What do you say? You will say one of three things.

You might say, "No! You demanded your money and thought you were smart enough to make it out there in the real world. But it wasn't so easy, was it, Hot Shot? I hope you learned your lesson. But there's no way you're coming back home. You've made your bed, so now you have to sleep in it."

Or you might say, "Maybe. But you'll come back only on my terms. You've blown it, and you have to prove yourself all over again. You want to be one of the servants? Okay, but you'll have to do all the dirty work. I want you to feed the pigs, milk the cows, clean the barn, and service the outhouse. If you can meet my standards, you might earn your way back to sonship."

Or you might say what the father in the parable said: "Welcome home! I've missed you terribly. Here's a robe, a ring, and some sandals. Let's have a party and invite everyone over to celebrate our reunion."

Which of those three responses do you think is the most common? I can guarantee you it is one of the first two. That third response is so full of acceptance that it is almost unthinkable to us. But it is the response that the father in the story chose. Even after his son had lost his superstar status and shown just how ordinary and sinful he really was, the father loved him anyway.

4. *The father didn't try to change either son, though both obviously needed changing.* The prodigal's motivation to change, notice carefully, came from *within* himself. Out there in the far country, Jesus tells us, "he came to his senses" (Luke 15:17). The father never once suggested an improvement program for him. There is no mention in the parable of harping, criticizing, or any of the other things we parents are prone to do to whip our kids into shape.

The older brother was treated the same way. Even after he revealed his selfish character, the father didn't try to change him. He just affirmed his love for the boy and reminded him that everything the father owned was his as well.

Not one of the techniques we often use to goad people to change was used by the father. He didn't put on a halo and parade his own goodness before his sons. He didn't lay a bunch of guilt on them and banish them to the doghouse. He didn't mirror their attitudes back to them and treat them the way they had treated him. He didn't throw a tantrum to try to get their attention. And he didn't flog them publicly by talking of their sins and holding them up to ridicule. The father was smart enough to know that change always arises from *within*, and that all of those old tricks wouldn't work.

5. *The father forgave the prodigal son, even though the boy was guilty.* The story is, first and foremost, a story about forgiveness. The father refused to keep score in his relationship with his son, and welcomed him back even though the boy was not worthy of such a gracious welcome. The father, bear in mind, *had* been wronged. He had been treated shabbily by his own flesh-and-blood and had every reason to be resentful and unforgiving. But he chose to forgive, and that choice opened the door of reconciliation that his son eventually walked through.

6. *The father's love was "narrow" and expressed in specific ways.* What the father did in Jesus' story is a model of "particular love." The father was straining his eyes to see only one person coming back home down that road. And when he saw him, he poured specific attention upon him. He put a ring on his finger, a robe on his back, and sandals on his feet. He had a party in his honor. Everything that was done was done for one solitary person— that wayward son who had come home.

This was probably what made the older brother so upset. He assumed "narrow" love was synonymous with "exclusive" love and felt left out. But the father was quick to assure him that he was valued too, that his love was big enough to embrace both sons.

7. *The father expressed his affection by touching his prodigal son.* When he saw that boy trudging home, the father ran to greet him, threw his arms around him, and kissed him. Before he ever said a word to his son, the father

assured him of his love by touching him. As I mentioned earlier, touch is the most intimate of the five senses, so the father broke down the barrier of estrangement with two simple tools: a hug and a kiss.

8. *The father renewed the relationship with a celebration.* When his son came home, the father threw a party. There was music. People danced, told jokes, and laughed until their sides hurt. It was scandalous, really, and the older boy was embarrassed by the merriment. He remembered all those nights that his father had spent pacing the floor and weeping over the prodigal's departure. It just didn't make sense that when the source of all of that pain finally returned, he would be greeted with festivity. The scene in the living room was just too much for the older brother to take: the father pounding the wayward son on the back and cackling over a funny story, tears of joy rolling down his cheeks.

But if the prodigal had any doubts about his father's love, they were banished at the party. When he laughed with his father, when he saw the joy in his father's eyes, he knew for certain that he was really home.

## A Plan for Loving Relationships

If those eight relational concepts have a familiar ring to them, it is only because I have spent the previous eight chapters in this book outlining them for you. The strategy for making our collisions more tender that I have sketched for you in these pages comes from the father in the parable of the prodigal. His kind of love seems to me to be the best model any of us could find.

It is not, however, the only model available to us, or even the only model in Jesus' story. The older brother also provides a possible model for relating to people. Stand those eight concepts on their head and you have the relational strategy of the older brother. He was full of self and demanded equal rights. He was angry at both his father and his brother and wasn't bashful about expressing his hostility. He wouldn't accept his brother and was even contemptuous of his father's acceptance of his brother. He wanted to change everybody but himself; he wanted his brother to clean up his act and his father to be more judgmental. He was unforgiving and eaten up with "scorekeeping." He didn't love anyone narrowly—except himself! He didn't want to hug or kiss anybody. And he certainly didn't feel like dancing or laughing at somebody's stupid jokes. Take those eight negative concepts and you have the older brother's philosophy of personal relationships. You also have a philosophy that is extremely popular to this very day.

But still the father's kind of love beckons to us. And the father's kind of love is the philosophy of relationships I've been trying to convey in this book. We don't have to relate to people the way the older brother did. We can opt for the father's kind of love, make our collisions tender, and spend most of our lives celebrating with people.

Let me put all eight of those relational principles together now, so you can see the philosophy of tender collisions in a summary package. Here's what they never told us about how to get along with each other:

- We can make our collisions tender if we will deny self and consider the needs of another before our own.

- We can make our collisions tender if we will refrain from any outbursts of anger that will wound other people.

- We can make our collisions tender if we will quit expecting people to be superstars and give them permission to be ordinary.

- We can make our collisions tender if we will quit trying to change people and give them the freedom to be different from us.

- We can make our collisions tender if we will quit keeping score and try to forgive others.

- We can make our collisions tender if we will narrow our focus and love a few people in specific ways.

- We can make our collisions tender if we will learn the importance of touch and make touching a natural part of our relationships.

- We can make our collisions tender if we will loosen up and laugh with people.

Those eight ideas sketch for us a new way of relating to others, a way in harmony with the Father's kind of love.

## Beyond Psychology

What most excites me about this strategy for our relationships is that it takes the best insights from modern culture and popular psychology, but then moves us *beyond* them. While it affirms certain popular ideas—the need for touch, the benefits of laughter, and the importance of acceptance, to mention three—it also prods us to be different than the masses. In particular, the Father's kind of love has less self and more grace than we are accustomed to. If we choose to adopt this strategy as our own, we will find ourselves becoming less selfish and more gracious in our relationships.

The Father's kind of love will make us, first, less selfish. Because it is built on the foundation of self-denial, this strategy will place us at odds with the popular way of doing relationships. We have been not-so-subtly taught that we are to fulfill self, glorify self, and even worship self. And much popular psychology underscores our tendency to place self on the throne of the universe.

Paul Vitz in his book *Psychology As Religion* reminds us of the difference in popular love and the Father's kind of love:

> It should be obvious—though it has apparently not been so to many—that the relentless and single-minded search for and glorification of the self is at direct cross-purposes with the Christian injunction to *lose* the self. Certainly Jesus Christ neither lived nor advocated a life that would qualify by today's standards as "self-actualized." For the Christian, self is the problem, not the potential paradise. Understanding this problem involves an awareness of sin, especially the sin of pride; correcting this condition requires the practice of such unself-actualized states as contrition and penitence, humility, obedience, and trust in God.

Certainly those qualities—awareness of sin, contrition, humility, obedience, and trust in God—are not in vogue these days. But because the Father's kind of love is built on self-denial instead of self-deification, those of us who choose this style of relating to others will find ourselves moving in the direction of those very qualities. We will quit asking, "How can I get my self actualized?"

and begin asking the revolutionary question that focuses on the needs of someone else.

The Father's kind of love will also make us more gracious. Those eight principles in our strategy for tender collisions just overflow with grace. It is grace that prompts us to deny self. It is grace that nudges us to withhold our anger. It is grace that enables us to accept and love non-superstars. It is grace that reminds us that changing people is not our business. It is grace that motivates us to forgive people. It is grace that narrows our love and particularizes our attention. It is grace that prompts us to touch others in loving ways. And it is grace that enables us to laugh. It is grace, you see, that energizes this whole strategy.

But grace has never been in vogue either. The reigning ethic in society has always been "an eye for an eye and a tooth for a tooth." And our culture is certainly no exception. We loudly declare our "rights" and pledge revenge on anyone who infringes upon them. We expect our family and friends to "meet our needs" and get hurt when they can't, or won't, comply. We feel it is our duty to go halfway in a relationship and no further. In short, we live graceless lives. But the Father's kind of love moves us in a radically new direction. It calls us to turn the other cheek, go the second mile, and return good for evil. Anyone who opts for such a strategy will look weird in an eye-for-an-eye culture.

Because these eight principles make us less selfish and more gracious, they move us beyond popular notions for relating to others. They make us less like the masses and more like the Father.

If anyone should ever ask you where you get your model for relating to people, I hope you'll point them to the Father in Jesus' famous story. But since the chances are good that no one will ever ask you such a question, I hope you'll just love like the Father. If you do, your life will offer a testimony far more compelling than your words ever could.

# 11

# *The Necessary Confrontation*

*Sometimes avoiding confrontation can cause more grief than confrontation does. As painful as it is to confront someone about a problem, not confronting that person can produce even more pain.*

*T*his chapter must be, sad to say, a strong dose of reality. I have spent this entire book telling you how to avoid hurt and hassle in your relationships. The eight relational principles I have discussed will take us to a new level of intimacy with people and will greatly reduce the number of abrasive collisions we have.

But into every life there inevitably comes a situation that calls for confrontation. The reality I want us to consider in this chapter is *how we confront people in a way that can make those collisions more tender.* When all else fails, when we have done all the right things and a relationship is still going sour, how do we handle the situation? How do we tell our child her behavior is unacceptable? How do we tell our employee his work must improve?

How do we approach the neighbor whose loud music is keeping us awake at night?

I myself run from such confrontations as often as possible. Given a choice between "fight" and "flight," I will nearly always opt for the latter. But occasionally I must remind myself that running from such encounters is not movement toward love; it is actually movement toward increased hostility. And occasionally I must also remind myself that being a part of God's kingdom is not the same as being a member of what David Seamands calls the "Dependent Order of Really Meek and Timid Souls" ("Doormats" for short). There are times when it is both good and necessary to confront a person about a problem.

## When to Confront

The first question we must ponder is: *When is it time to get confrontational?* How do we know when to remain silent and when to speak an assertive word? For me there are three times when it is important to confront a person, three times when silence is wrong in a relationship.

*First, it is time to confront a person when something which that person is doing is making us consistently angry.* Anger left untended festers into a resentment that can destroy a relationship. It is much better to address the issue that is prompting that anger than it is to suffer in silence while the relationship slowly turns bitter. Confronting a person in this kind of situation is like lancing a boil: For all the pain involved, it is still healthier than having to endure long-term misery.

I have already spent an entire chapter on the destruction caused when we vent our hostility on someone, and you know by now that I'm not an advocate of exploding on people to make us feel better. Most of the time silence really is golden in our relationships, and we definitely don't have to verbalize our feelings every time we get angry.

But there are times when someone does something that bothers us—the teacher regularly screams at our son in class, the employee is late every day, the next-door neighbor's dog gets in our trash at least twice a week— and to ignore this bothersome behavior will only make us more resentful toward that person. In other words, the only way the relationship can be improved is to confront the person with the problem and hope it can be resolved. To fail to confront is to guarantee that the relationship will never get better.

Of course there is risk in such confrontation. The teacher may tell us all the reasons our son *needs* to be scolded. The employee may get huffy and quit. And the next-door neighbor might be obliged to tell us about the havoc our cat is wreaking at *their* house. But those risks are worth taking if we want to enhance our relationship with those people.

*Second, it is time to confront a person when that person's actions are hurting other people.* The problem with problems is that they are never isolated. Problems and sins inevitably have ripples, and they inflict damage on innocent bystanders. When we see that someone's sin or negligence is inflicting pain upon others, that person must be confronted.

The air traffic controller with the drinking problem needs to be confronted, or else innocent travelers might lose their lives. The abusive parent needs to be confronted, or else innocent children might get hurt. The preacher carrying on a clandestine affair needs to be confronted, or else innocent church members might suffer. The incompetent doctor needs to be confronted, or else dozens of innocent patients might experience grief because of his incompetency. Whenever we see that the sins of one person are affecting the lives of others, it is time to step forward with an assertive word.

I think this is the key to understanding Jesus' outburst of anger when he cleansed the temple. We usually think of Jesus as meek and mild, but on this occasion he took a whip in his hands and got downright confrontive! He overturned tables and chased the moneychangers from the temple area. Gentle Jesus meek and mild was transformed into a tiger that day.

Why? What prompted such assertiveness? I think it has something to do with the very point I'm trying to make here. Jesus confronted these moneychangers because their greed was ruining worship for many innocent worshipers. Think of the scene: men chanting like carnival barkers trying to woo people to their booths to have their foreign money changed into Galilean shekels—for a fee, of course! Coins clattering on the tables and floors. Doves fluttering in cages, waiting to be sold as sacrifices. All in all, it was a chaotic scene punctuated by the raucous noise of greedy businessmen trying to turn a quick buck in the name of religion.

Imagine what it would have been like if one worshiper had wanted to spend some quiet time at the temple that day. One fisherman fresh from a long night at sea. Or one housewife tired of being mother to a household of screaming kids. This fisherman or this housewife slips off to seek the presence of God at the temple but is greeted by chaos and greed and carnival barkers. And that, I think, is why Jesus got so angry. The sins of the moneychangers were trampling on the rights of the fisherman and housewife. The problems of the businessmen were making problems for innocent seekers who just wanted to catch a glimpse of God at the temple. Whenever such things happen, whenever the sins of one person or one group spill over onto others, confrontation is in order. The pain of confronting one person over a problem is insignificant when compared to the pain that others will experience if the problem is ignored.

*Third, it is time to confront a person when that person's actions are damaging himself.* There has evolved now in certain counseling centers a process known as "intervention." In intervention, family members and loved ones confront a person about a problem such as drug or alcohol abuse. It is a painful confrontation, an emotional collision that any normal person would not relish. But in some cases it is necessary because it forces the drug or alcohol abuser to see the problem and to realize the damage which the problem is causing.

Intervention is necessary because that person has become blind to his problem. And that blindness can strike anyone. As I said earlier, we are all better at seeing the speck in our brother's eye than we are at detecting the log that is in our own. But if my blindness ever becomes so acute that I am doing great harm to myself, the kindest thing you could do for me is confront me and try to help me see. Do it kindly, gently, humbly. But if you really care for me, do it.

That last sentence is, of course, the key to this kind of confrontation. We must truly care for someone and want that person to know joy in order to confront him. Frankly, we will never confront a stranger about such problems. In the first place, we don't know the stranger well enough to perceive the magnitude of the problem. And in the second place, we don't love the stranger enough to care if he is hurting himself. Real, personal love always precedes this third reason for confrontation, and while we like to say we are nonconfrontive because we don't want to hurt feelings, it is possible that we are nonconfrontive because we don't really care.

I'm reminded of something that Carol Bly wrote in her book *Letters from the Country*. The book is about small-town life in Minnesota, and Bly comments on the polite nonconfrontation that prevents intimacy:

> The case is always made that to keep a town from flying apart you must discuss only matters in which there is little conflict. That means that whenever a woman physician enters a room in which a few people are urging, intriguingly enough, that the man should be head of the woman (St. Paul), the topic must automatically be changed to whether or not we are getting that hard winter they kept talking about last fall.
>
> There is nothing much wrong with weather talk except that far from preventing people from feeling "threatened" it is in fact the living proof that you don't care about those people: you haven't any interest in their thoughts; you don't want to hear them out.

In other words, honest dialogue and gentle confrontation are statements of caring. If we truly care for someone, we can't sit idly by while that person damages himself. Love demands that we kindly confront.

The key factor in all three of these ideas can be expressed like this: We should be assertive and confrontive if something important is at stake, and more will be gained than lost in the confrontation. Determining that fact is not easy, of course, and it always comes down to a personal judgment call. But these are the three questions that can help us decide when to confront someone: 1) Will the confrontation make my relationship with this person better? 2) Will the confrontation ease the pain of some innocent sufferers? 3) Will the confrontation lessen the damage this person is inflicting upon himself?

If the answer to any of those three questions is yes, it is time to confront.

### How to Confront

Still lurking in the shadows, though, is the hardest question of all: *How* do I confront people? Even if our timing is perfect, our confrontations will be anything but tender if we don't know how to confront. Again, I have developed a personal philosophy that includes three key ingredients. If we could consistently put these three ideas into practice, I think we could make even our unpleasant clashes more tender.

*First, confront directly.* This is the most difficult part of any confrontation, and we will bypass it whenever possible. But any honest, ethical confrontation must be direct.

In his fine book on leadership, *Love and Profit*, James Autry tells of a problem that arose in a rural high school. One of the teachers in the school was wearing exceedingly revealing clothes, and her inappropriate dress was causing classroom problems with the teenaged male students.

The superintendent of schools got wind of the problem and told the principal to speak to the teacher about the teachers' dress code. About two weeks passed, and the situation was no better. The principal called the superintendent to ask what to do next.

"Did you speak with her?" the superintendent asked. "Yes," the principal replied, but later the superintendent found out that the principal had actually called a faculty meeting and addressed the subject to the entire group. He didn't confront the teacher directly.

That, of course, is the easiest way to handle such a problem. Keep the confrontation general, and no one is offended. But such confrontation wastes the time of innocent teachers, makes them wonder why they should be berated for the sins of another person, and allows the guilty teacher to think that since everyone is catching the heat, she's probably safe. Better, though harder, to seek the teacher out one-on-one and tell her about the concern.

The most honest and effective confrontation is the direct one. If you have a problem with your child's teacher, don't go to the principal; go to the teacher. If that meeting doesn't accomplish what you want it to accomplish, then go to the principal. If you have a problem with a fellow employee, don't go to your boss; go to the employee and speak your piece. If you think your pastor has committed some grievous wrong, don't air your complaints to the church board; go to the pastor personally.

If we would adopt the strategy that all future confrontations would be direct, we would reap two delightful dividends: 1) our complaints would decline in number because direct confrontations are so difficult to initiate, and 2) the amount of gossip, hurt feelings, and back-biting in our relationships would decline too, because direct confrontation prevents us from talking about others behind their back.

*Second, confront thoughtfully.* By that I mean give the confrontation some thought. This is probably the main reason our confrontations fail. We speak off the cuff, often in anger, and the relationship is damaged instead of enhanced.

Thoughtful confrontation enables us to keep anger out of a relationship. Angry confrontation inevitably produces humiliation, hurt feelings, and estrangement. Anger is too easily used as a weapon when we confront someone, and it is a weapon that leaves destruction in its wake.

Instead of confronting someone when you're angry, don't say anything until you give the confrontation some thought. Pray about what you should say. Write some ideas on paper. Maybe even write a letter detailing your feelings, and take that letter with you when you talk to the person. But if the relationship means anything to you at all, don't deal with any problem off the cuff.

The general rule of thumb is: Thoughtless confrontations lead to hostility; thoughtful confrontations lead to reconciliation.

*Third, confront kindly.* We always need to keep in mind that the purpose of confrontation is reconciliation. We go into the confrontation with the sole intent of making our relationship better with that particular person.

That may seem obvious, but it is equally obvious that we don't approach most of our confrontations with reconciliation in mind. Instead, we go with self-justification in mind. Or revenge. Or condemnation. And, as with nearly everything else in life, we get what we aim for. After the confrontation we feel justified, vengeful, or smugly condemning. But sadly, we are farther from reconciliation after the confrontation than we were before.

Autry says there is one question he uses when he is in conflict with another person:

> The useful question is a simple technique I learned a long time ago and have used many times. It never fails. When the disagreement or conflict reaches a point that seems an impasse, I ask, "What would you like me to do?"
>
> The first reaction is astonishment. Then I elaborate, "If I could do anything to make this situation okay in your eyes, what would that be?"

That is the attitude with which we should approach every confrontation. We are not launching a verbal attack. We are not trying to belittle a person. We are not trying to prove our point of view. And we are not trying to make ourselves feel better by venting some hostility. We are trying to move closer to someone, to bridge the gulf that is separating us from that person. If we go into a confrontation with that purpose in mind, the chances are good that the collision can actually improve the relationship.

Those three simple ideas define, at least for me, the proper way to confront a person: Confront directly, confront thoughtfully, and confront kindly. If we would follow those three simple guidelines, even our unpleasant collisions would become more tender.

## The Rhythm of Reconciliation

Conflict in itself is neither good nor bad; it all depends on what you and I do with it. Conflict is good to the extent that it fosters reconciliation. It is bad to the extent that it fosters estrangement. And knowing when and how to confront people determines which direction our conflicts go.

The Bible has quite a few things to say about conflict and confrontation. In fact, if you will look at Jesus with new eyes, you will realize just how confrontive he was. While we like to think of Jesus as meek and mild, he often asserted himself and challenged people. The cleansing of the temple, as I mentioned, is one notable example. He also confronted the Pharisees about their hypocrisy. He confronted his followers about their apathy. He confronted Simon Peter when he suggested that Jesus would not have to die. He confronted the rich young ruler about his materialism. And even today, when we read the words of Jesus in the Gospels we are confronted with the rigorous demands of real discipleship. "Gentle Jesus meek and mild" just doesn't square with the Gospel record of who he really was.

In the Sermon on the Mount Jesus gave us a pattern for handling confrontations, a kind of rhythm that will lead to reconciliation. In Matthew 5:23,24 we learn of this rhythm that can make our relationships better.

*"If you are offering your gift at the altar . . ."* Life is going along smoothly. We're involved in routine things: school, work, ball games, church. Life is good, with hardly a ripple on the sea of our tranquility.

*". . . and there remember that your brother has something against you . . ."* But then conflict comes. Somebody is angry at us. We've wronged our husband. We've screamed

at our son or daughter. We've gossiped about a co-worker. There at the altar we see our sin. The conflict comes into sharp focus. We know that one of our relationships is in jeopardy. And we have to decide how to handle it.

*"... leave your gift there in front of the altar. First go and be reconciled to your brother ..."* We decide to make that relationship a high priority and get things straight between us and the offended person. We take some initiative. We seek the person out. We apologize for our part in the conflict. We ask James Autry's question: "What would you like me to do?" We tell the person, too, what he has done to hurt us. We directly, thoughtfully, and kindly confront the person with the problem that is hurting the relationship. Ideally, the relationship is restored, even made stronger by the confrontation.

*"... then come and offer your gift."* Now we can start living with joy again. Since we have restored our relationship with the person, we can approach God with a new peace in our heart. There is nothing that would hinder intimacy with him. Once again, life is good. We have taken the initiative to be reconciled to the person we have been in conflict with, and we can get on with living.

There is, of course, the possibility that our meeting with the person will not lead to the intimacy we desire. We can confront directly, thoughtfully, and kindly and still not achieve reconciliation.

Later on in the Gospel of Matthew, Jesus acknowledges this possibility and tells us what to do in such a situation. In Matthew 18:15-17 he tells us to confront the person one-on-one about the problem that is damaging the relationship. If that doesn't work, he says to take a few friends and try again. If even that doesn't work, he says to broaden the circle of concerned people and try again. And if even that doesn't work—if you have unsuccessfully tried everything possible to be reconciled to the person—then "treat him as you would a pagan or a tax collector" (Matthew 18:17). In other words, don't sweat it anymore!

That thought may seem rather harsh, but actually it is very liberating. Jesus is acknowledging that one person can only do so much in the reconciling process. If we have done everything possible to restore a relationship but the other person won't respond to our kindness, we can't do any more. So we shouldn't drown in guilt, and we shouldn't harbor resentment. Instead, we should move on down the road of life, staying open to the possibility that the "pagan or tax collector" will someday respond to our offer of reconciliation.

## Life in Nazareth and Capernaum

One day Jesus decided to return to his boyhood home of Nazareth. Was it to see old faces and renew old ties? To eat in the homes of boyhood chums and visit the synagogue where he had first studied about God? Would there be a homecoming of celebration and nostalgia?

When he went home to Nazareth, Jesus went to worship in the synagogue, read a passage from Isaiah 61, declared himself the fulfillment of that passage about the Messiah—and promptly angered everybody present. Luke records that "the people in the synagogue were furious when they heard this. They got up, drove him out of the town, and took him to the brow of the hill on which the town was built, in order to throw him down the cliff" (Luke 4:28,29). Some homecoming celebration! Fortunately, Jesus was able to escape and went from Nazareth to Capernaum.

His experience at Capernaum was completely different. After his rejection at Nazareth, he moved right on down the road and found the people of Capernaum more than receptive to his message. "They were amazed at his teaching, because his message had authority" (Luke 4:32). Then Jesus performed a miraculous healing, and the people were amazed at his power. Luke says, "The news about him spread throughout the surrounding area" (Luke 4:37).

What a difference! Rejection and near-death in his hometown of Nazareth, miracles and adulation in nearby Capernaum. Jesus experienced the agony of rejection in one place and the ecstasy of acceptance in another.

Chances are that we will have this same experience ourselves. We will have some "Nazareth" days, days when conflict is in the air and anger runs rampant. If Jesus' experience in his hometown proves anything at all, it proves that even good people sometimes run into conflict. But we will also have some "Capernaum" days, days when we feel loved and accepted and people are wonderful to us. We all must live at times in Nazareth, and we all must live at times in Capernaum.

The trick is not to let the disappointment at Nazareth keep us from making the journey to Capernaum. We can't let a few bad relationships and tragic conflicts close us up to the possibilities of new love down the road.

### Testimony of a Doormat

I once got caught squarely in the middle of a squabble. Good Christian people had an honest difference of opinion. I was their pastor and knew they were at odds with one another. It was one of those situations that called for a redemptive handling of conflict. It was a time for loving confrontation.

But I resisted. I hoped and prayed that things would work out without my intervention. I tried to steer clear of controversy and did my best to play ostrich-in-the-sand. But my do-nothing policy, I'm sad to say, exploded in my face. People got hurt. The church suffered. But I learned a needed lesson the hard way: Sometimes avoiding confrontation can cause more grief than confrontation does. As painful as it is to confront someone about a problem, not confronting that person can produce even more pain.

It is out of that kind of real-life experience that I offer you the ideas in this chapter. If you will follow the relational principles I have offered in the previous chapters, I think you'll find life a lot smoother. But if and when you have to confront someone, do it and do it well.

I think I can sum up the ideas in this chapter in three simple sentences.

First, there is a right time for confrontation. Know when that time is, and don't confront on a whim or in a fit of rage.

Second, there is a right approach to confrontation. Know how to confront so that the relationship can be repaired, so that reconciliation can take place.

And third, there is a right response when loving confrontation fails. Know that you can only do so much in any relationship, and take heart that just down the road from Nazareth is Capernaum!

# 12

# *Why the Rich Get Richer*

*Those who have learned the right way to invest their lives, those who have learned the right system, will grow richer and richer. Those who have learned the wrong way to invest their lives, those who have learned a faulty system, will grow poorer and poorer. It may not seem fair, but it is the way life works.*

Stephen Brown in his book <u>No More Mr. Nice Guy!</u> tells the story of a man who wanted to build a birdhouse. The man ordered plans for the birdhouse and looked forward to constructing it and putting it in his backyard.

The plans eventually arrived in the mail, and the man launched into his building project. Quickly he discovered, though, that a mistake had been made. The company had inadvertently sent him the plans for a sailboat. He wrote the company a letter explaining the problem and got a letter of apology in reply.

The company said that his request had gotten mixed up with some other requests and that the mistake would be corrected. In the last line of the letter the company representative wrote, "However, if you think you had problems with your birdhouse, you ought to see the man who ordered plans for a sailboat. He says that his new boat looks funny and that it won't float."

That story underscores our dilemma when it comes to building quality relationships: Many of us are simply building by the wrong pattern. We have assumed that our blueprint is accurate and will help us construct good and sturdy relationships. But the truth is that we're trying to build from the wrong set of instructions. And we are finding out, much to our chagrin, that it is nearly impossible to sail through life in a birdhouse.

## Why the Rich Get Richer...

A man once had to take a journey. Before that journey he called three of his workers into his office and gave each of them a sum of money to safeguard in his absence. He gave one worker 5000 dollars. He gave another 2000 dollars. And he gave the third worker 1000 dollars. He then left on his trip, and each worker had to decide what to do with his money.

The first worker invested his money wisely and doubled his 5000 dollars. The second worker also doubled his money. The third worker, though, was the cautious, play-it-close-to-the-vest type and buried his 1000 dollars in the ground.

When the man returned from his trip, each worker had to give an account of his money. The first worker gleefully reported that he had doubled the money entrusted to him, and the owner praised him for his shrewd investment. The second worker also reported that he had doubled his money, and he too received the master's praise. The third worker candidly confessed what he had done: "Master, I knew that you are a hard man, harvesting where you have not sown and gathering where you have not scattered seed. So I was afraid and went out and hid your money in the ground. See, here is what belongs to you" (Matthew 25:24,25). The man was furious at this worker's caution and even called him "wicked" and "lazy."

What happens next seems strange to us. The angry owner takes the thousand dollars from this third worker and gives it to the worker who has the ten thousand. And evidently this is the primary truth of the parable, for Jesus then offers this summary statement: "For everyone who has will be given more, and he will have an abundance. Whoever does not have, even what he has will be taken from him" (Matthew 25:29).

Does that seem fair to you? Does it seem right that the rich man should get richer and the poor man should have even his small bit of money snatched away from him? Well, before we rise up in righteous indignation against Jesus' unfair labor practices, we need to know that he is reminding us here of a law that is true in every area of life. Those who have learned the right way to invest their lives, those who have learned the right "system," will grow richer and richer. Those who have learned the wrong way to invest their lives, those who have learned a faulty "system," will grow poorer and poorer. It may not seem fair, but it _is_ the way life works.

And nowhere is the truth of Jesus' parable more obvious than in the area of personal relationships. Those who learn how to love, how to build intimacy, how to collide tenderly will find their relationships getting better and better. Conversely, those who don't learn how to build quality relationships will find their relationships a constant source of frustration. They will be like that poor guy whose sailboat just wouldn't float, because they have built their relationships by the wrong pattern. Eventually even what little intimacy they have will be taken away from them.

What I have tried to do in this book is show you a new system for our relationships, a system that I think will help us become richer and richer. If we begin to live the ideas in this book, we will set in motion a positive cycle that will enrich our relationships and lead us to a new level of relational intimacy and personal joy.

## Retaking the Test

In Chapter 1 of this book I invited you to take a quick test on relating to people. I made nine statements and asked you to agree or disagree with each of them. Then I said that there was a flaw in each statement, a flaw that just might be sabotaging your attempt to build relationships that are loving and lasting.

Now that I have proposed to you a new system for relating to others, let's look at that test again and see the fatal flaw in each of those statements.

1. *The most important ingredient we can bring to a relationship is healthy self-esteem.*
Granted, we all want and need a good biblical self-image, for this is a boon to relationships. But even more important than self-*esteem* is self-*denial*. There are thousands of people who "feel good about themselves" but

still have lousy relationships. We will never be satisfied in our relationships until we move beyond self-*esteem* to embrace self-*denial*. The most important ingredient we can bring to a relationship is the willingness to deny self and to serve others.

**2.** *It is healthy and good to express anger to another person.*
Actually, it is usually destructive and bad to express anger to another person. The "let-it-all-hang-out" philosophy of our day has done untold damage to millions of relationships. When we vent our hostility on another person, we run the risk of doing irreparable harm to that person. Words can inflict deep wounds and leave indelible scars.

**3.** *We should always expect supreme effort and high achievement from the people around us.*
Well . . . yes and no. While it is certainly true that high expectation can call out the best in people, the above statement easily translates into rewarding only the superstars in our world. It smacks of "I will accept you if you measure up," and it leaves ordinary people desperate for acknowledgment. There are many times when effort will not be supreme and achievement will not be high, and we will have to love ordinary people in their imperfection.

**4.** *A parent's job is to keep a child from failing and to make sure that child becomes successful.*
No, a parent cannot keep a child from failing. Nor can a parent insure a child's success in life. If we parents assume we can do those things, we will try to change our children, make them in our image, and manipulate their

lives. It is quite possible, you see, that "square peg" parents can have "round hole" children, and those parents must allow their kids the freedom to be different than they are. It is not a parent's job to mold a child into a certain image; it is a parent's job to create a relationship of grace and trust where a child can become what he or she wants to become.

5. *We should always be fair in our dealings with people.*
This statement is perhaps a bit underhanded and tricky. Of course we should be fair in our dealings with people. But what I want you to see is that quality relationships are always built on something more than fairness. They are built on *grace*, and grace is not fair. If we are always fair in our dealings with people, our relationships will be poor. Fairness doesn't turn the other cheek, go the second mile, or love an enemy, but Jesus advocates all of those practices in the Sermon on the Mount. And what the prodigal son got when he came back home was not *fairness* but *grace*. The older brother wanted the father to be fair, but the father knew that only *grace* could guarantee reconciliation with his wayward son. Treat people fairly, and those people will respect you. Treat people graciously, and those people will love you.

6. *The more people we love, the better.*
If we believe that statement, it probably means our understanding of love is shallow. Love, to be love, must be narrow in its focus and specific in its action. Quality relationships are not built by scatter-shooting nice deeds on a bunch of people but by concentrating love on a special few.

**7.** *We best communicate our love to people by telling them we love them.*

It is wonderful, and even necessary, to speak our affection to others. But it is even more necessary to communicate our love to people by touching them. Since touch is the most intimate of the five senses, it is also the most intimate way to express our affection. By all means, tell people you love them. But if you never touch them, your words are mostly in vain.

**8.** *Any relationship can be rejuvenated if we will take it seriously.*

Again, this is a tricky way to make the point, but it would be truer to say: Any relationship can be rejuvenated if we will take it *humorously.* The way to grow closer to people is to laugh with them. Laughter not only heals diseased bodies, but it also heals damaged relationships.

**9.** *We learn to love better by studying psychology and finding out the intricacies of the human psyche.*

Psychology, for all its benefits, cannot teach us how to love. In fact, it can actually keep us *from* love if we use it to focus our attention on self. To the degree that psychology keeps us from self-denial, it prevents us from building loving relationships. The best model for our relationships doesn't come from any psychologist or psychological theory; it comes from the New Testament and its picture of a loving Father. The Father's kind of love, the kind of love I've been trying to capture in this book, is the finest model we have available to us.

## Is It Easy or Hard?

Perhaps as you've read this book you have found yourself agreeing with the ideas I've mentioned here. You believe that this system would lead to successful relationships, but you also believe that this system is impractical and even impossible.

Your protest, if you were to try to put it in words, might go something like this: "This all sounds well and good, but I just don't think I can pull it off. It's easy to talk about not losing your temper, for example, but I just can't keep from getting mad sometimes. It's easy to say we should accept ordinary people, not try to change them, and forgive them of their wrongs, but I get terribly frustrated at some of the people I'm supposed to love. God may be able to relate to people this way, but I just can't. As nice as your system sounds, I just don't think it will work for people like me. It's too hard."

Is it too hard? I think of something Eugene Peterson wrote in his book *A Long Obedience in the Same Direction*:

> The easiest thing in the world is to be a Christian. What is hard is to be a sinner. Being a Christian is what we were created for. The life of faith has the support of an entire creation and the resources of a magnificent redemption. The structure of this world was created by God so we could live in it easily and happily as his children. The history we walk in has been repeatedly entered by God, most notably in Jesus Christ, first to show us and then to help us live full of faith and exuberant with purpose. In the course of Christian discipleship we discover that without Christ we were

doing it the hard way and that with Christ we are doing it the easy way. It is not Christians who have it hard, but non-Christians.

That's exactly the way I feel about the ideas I've presented in this book. The easiest thing in the world is to begin relating to people this way, to fall in step with the way God intended us to relate to people in the first place. What is hard is to live your whole life estranged from people. What is hard is to have a constant knot in your stomach because of a bad marriage. What is hard is to be upset with your kids all the time. What is hard is to dread going to work every day because your relationships at the office are so deplorable. What is hard is to live your life by a pattern guaranteed to keep you in consistent conflict with other people.

Imagine, if you can, a minor league baseball player who bats cross-handed. This particular player "has all the tools," as they say in baseball lingo. He can field, run, and throw. But early in life he learned to bat cross-handed, and now batting the proper way feels unnatural to him. Coaches have tried to convince him that he'll never be much of a hitter until he learns to bat with the conventional grip. But he says it's just too hard to change now, that he'd have to learn how to bat all over again if he changed his familiar grip.

So he continues to knock around in the minor leagues and will in fact never make it to the majors as long as he bats cross-handed. Oh, occasionally he gets a base hit, but he doesn't have much power and his average hovers around .200. He is doomed to a frustrating existence in the minor leagues, but still refuses to change his batting style.

Now I ask you: Is it really too hard for him to change? If he wants to start hitting the ball with some authority, shouldn't he swallow his pride and learn to hit the right way? If he wants to achieve his lifelong dream of making the majors, shouldn't he go ahead and alter his grip? And which is harder, changing his batting style or being condemned to a frustrating career as a minor league player?

Many of us, I'm afraid, are trying to make the major leagues using the wrong system. We want to be closer to our family. We want to have more intimacy. We want to make friends. But we're trying to hit homers in our relationships using the wrong grip. What is truly hard is to stubbornly refuse to change and to stay locked in a series of unsatisfying relationships. What is truly easy is to change and to begin to experience love.

## A Wake-Up Call

If we are currently floundering in relational misery, there are two likely reasons for it. First, our system is bad. That is, we have never learned how to relate to people, and we need to use some of the ideas in this book to alter our approach. Second, we've just grown careless. We know how to build quality relationships, but we've neglected the people in our lives. We have forgotten that intimacy can be lost if we don't tend to our relationships.

Bruce Larson in his book *The One and Only You* quotes his friend Art Sueltz, who once delineated the seven stages of a cold in the life of a young married couple:

> The first year the husband says: "Sugar, I'm worried about my little baby girl. You've got a bad sniffle. I want to put you in the hospital for

a complete checkup. I know the food is lousy, but I've arranged for your meals to be sent up from Rossini's. It's all arranged."

The second year: "Listen, honey, I don't like the sound of that cough. I've called Dr. Miller and he's going to rush right over. Now will you go to bed like a good girl just for me, please?"

Third year: "Maybe you'd better lie down, honey. Nothing like a little rest if you're feeling bad. I'll bring you something to eat. Have we got any soup in the house?"

Fourth year: "Look, dear. Be sensible. After you've fed the kids and washed the dishes you'd better hit the sack."

Fifth year: "Why don't you take a couple of aspirin?"

Sixth year: "If you'd just gargle or something instead of sitting around barking like a seal."

Seventh year: "For heaven's sake, stop sneezing. What are you trying to do, give me pneumonia?"

The fading affection pictured in those seven stages is funny to read about, but not so funny to experience. But there is more truth in Sueltz's declining progression than we care to admit. We neglect our relationships, and intimacy takes a gradual nosedive.

Certainly we don't intend for our relationships to slowly collapse. When we said "I do" at the altar that day, for instance, we envisioned a life of perpetual romance and growing love. But, like the husband mentioned above, the years have bred more apathy than romance.

When we peered in the nursery window at the hospital 16 years ago we were filled with awe at that miracle in
the crib who bore our name. What a kid! What promise
for the future! How could we ever have known that we
would one day be estranged from that miracle and find
him to be more pain than promise?

And when we began that job a few years back, we were
amazed that we could land such a position. The pay was
great, the people gracious. We started with such gratitude and expectancy. How could we have ever predicted
that we would one day dread going to work, that we
would feel such anger toward our co-workers?

The culprit in the demise of all of those relationships is
probably neglect. We just grew careless. We forgot to
court our spouse *after* the wedding. We let that 16-year-
old grow up without our careful attention. We let the
mechanics of doing our job overshadow the need to
nurture our relationships at work. And now we're paying the price. We're reaping what we've sowed. We're
mired in a myriad of declining relationships. And we
will *stay* mired in bad relationships until we do something to turn things around.

What shall we do? Install a new system, and begin to
pay more attention.

### Packing Your Own Lunch

I have never claimed to be much of a soothsayer, but
I'd like to make a prediction: If on our deathbed we have
opportunity to review our lives, our biggest regrets will
have to do with Jesus' Great Commandment. That is, we
will regret we didn't know God more intimately, and we
will regret we didn't know people more intimately. Perhaps we will feel remorse over some poor financial

investments we made, or an ill-advised decision to change jobs, or the move we made to a different city. But all of the remorse caused by such mistakes will not come close, I predict, to the remorse we will feel because we blew our chance at knowing God and loving people.

Now, here's the good news: We don't have to die with those regrets. We can begin *now* to focus on our spiritual condition, to make knowing and loving God our priority. And we can begin *now* to pay attention to the people in our lives and to employ a new system for relating to them. *Right now* we can assume responsibility for our relationships and build a future quite different from our past.

In his bestselling book *It Was on Fire When I Lay Down on It*, Robert Fulghum reports a conversation he had with a colleague. The man was complaining that he had the same old stuff in his lunch bag day after day.

"So who makes your lunch?" Fulghum asked.

"I do," replied the man.

When it comes to relationships, we all pack our own lunch. What I have tried to do in this book is suggest some fresh items you can put in your bag. I want you to know it doesn't have to be the same old stuff day after day. You have the power to change the way you treat people, make your collisions tender, and establish a network of loving relationships.

Let me leave you with this question: If you can have fried chicken and all the trimmings in your bag, why settle for a stale bologna sandwich?

# A
# *Closing*
# *Plea*

While I was writing this book, two incidents happened in my own front yard that underscored for me the sad condition of our society.

About a month ago I was in my driveway, putting seat covers in my minivan, when I heard someone screaming obscenities. I looked over at the elementary school across the street and saw a second- or third-grade boy trudging across the schoolyard toward a dilapidated car parked at the curb. A burly man was sitting in the car, and it was this man who was filling the air with cursing. The object of the swearing? The little boy, head down, book bag in hand, heading across the schoolyard!

I watched, panic-stricken and heartbroken, as the boy moved closer to the car. The man, whom I presume was the boy's father, continued to scream at him, calling him every name in the book. The man, I could tell by the screaming, had taken off work to pick up the boy, and the boy had not been at the right place. Once the boy got in the car, the father continued to verbally abuse him, and even as the car turned the corner and headed home I could still hear the cursing and name-calling. The question that haunted me most was this: If that little boy gets treated like that in *public*, what does he get in *private*?

Then just this past week a similar incident occurred. It was about eight o'clock in the morning, and parents were bringing their children to that same school across the street. Suddenly I heard crying and yelling. I walked out on the front porch to investigate and saw a little girl standing beside a car, crying. She was telling a woman in the car—her mother, I would guess—that she didn't want to go in by herself, that she wanted her to go with her. The mother screamed at the little girl, "If you get back in this car, I'll kill you!" The little girl started to shriek and sob louder, and the mother yelled this time, "If you get back in this car, I'll strangle you!" With that she stepped on the gas and left the little girl sobbing in the street.

Those two incidents, in my own front yard, still haunt me. I know that most parents get upset with their children and say things they eventually regret. But those two incidents were different: They were filled with anger and hate; they were abusive, relationship-destroying collisions that made me heartsick. What could those parents be thinking? How can those children survive such attacks? And will those children grow up screaming at their children, abusing them, heaping hate upon them?

I would like to think that those two episodes were rare occurrences, that those people were having bad days and will never again unleash that kind of venom on their kids. But I'm afraid that this is not the case. I'm afraid they regularly scream at their children, hit them, treat them like dirt. I'm afraid what I witnessed in my front yard goes on in thousands of families every day in our country. I'm afraid we are becoming more violent and less loving by the day.

But it doesn't have to be that way. We don't ever have to scream at people. We don't ever have to swear or hit or "lose our cool." We can be different. We can put into practice the "tender collision" ideas I've mentioned in this book and put an end to the kind of scenes I've just described.

In a world where abrasiveness and divisiveness run rampant, we can do what the apostle Paul encourages us to do in Colossians 3:12-14: "Therefore, as God's chosen people, holy and dearly loved, clothe yourselves with compassion, kindness, humility, gentleness and patience. Bear with each other and forgive whatever grievances you may have against one another. Forgive as the Lord forgave you. And over all these virtues put on love, which binds them all together in perfect unity."

With God's help let's do it!

# Other Good
# Harvest House Reading

## OVERCOMING HURTS AND ANGER
by *Dr. Dwight Carlson*

Dr. Carlson shows us how to confront our feelings and negative emotions in order to experience liberation and fulfillment. He presents seven practical steps to help us identify and cope with our feelings of hurt and anger.

## TOUGH TALK TO A STUBBORN SPOUSE
by *Stephen Schwambach*

In the United States, someone gets divorced every 27 seconds. Nine times out of ten, only one of the partners wants a divorce, and it's the same one every time: the stubborn one. You may be that person. Perhaps you are the other spouse, or a child, or a relative or friend, but your heart is breaking because someone for whom you care deeply is headed straight for a divorce. What can you do?

Now you can give your loved one *Tough Talk to a Stubborn Spouse*. Author Stephen Schwambach pours 20 years of counseling and pastoring stubborn people into short, powerful chapters that will stimulate the thinking of husbands or wives. It could be the key that unlocks a desperate situation as Schwambach leads the reader through a last, hard look at their marriage.

## SILENT STRENGTH FOR MY LIFE
by *Lloyd John Ogilvie*

*Gladness . . . refreshment . . . encouragement . . . renewal . . .* these are the rich rewards of quiet time spent with God. Daily time spent with God, alone in His presence, satisfied by His Word, makes our hearts stronger and our vision clearer. *Silent Strength* is designed to help you maximize your time with our Lord. As we glimpse His power, we find ourselves ready to meet the challenges of the day with a strength that is beyond our own, a silent strength that comes from God alone.